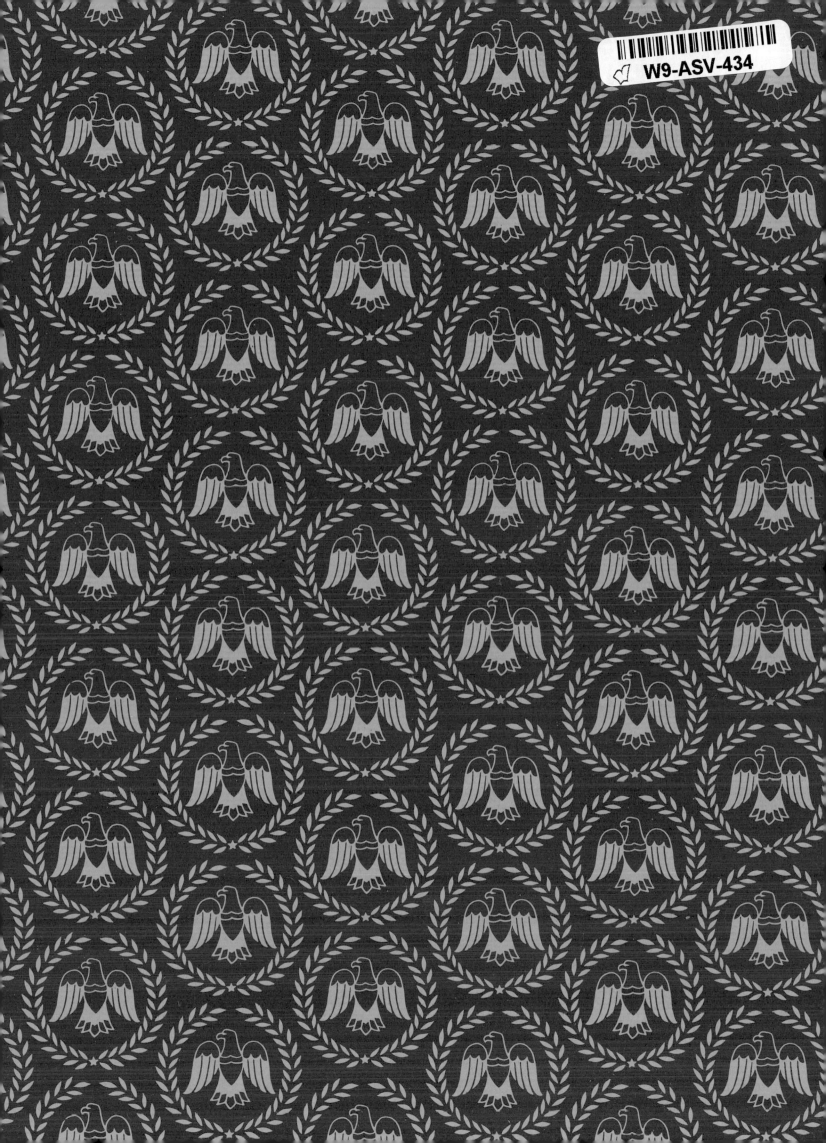

Treasury of American Design

TREASURY OF

OF

VOLUME TWO

A Pictorial Survey of Popular Folk Arts

Based upon Watercolor Renderings in the

Index of American Design, at the

National Gallery of Art

AMERICAN DESIGN

by Clarence P. Hornung

FOREWORD by J. CARTER BROWN
Director, National Gallery of Art, Washington, D.C.

INTRODUCTION by HOLGER CAHILL
Formerly National Director, Index of American Design

HARRY N. ABRAMS, INC., *Publishers*, NEW YORK

Standard Book Number: 8109–0516–7
Library of Congress Catalogue Card Number: 76–142742
All rights reserved. No part of the contents of this book may be
reproduced without the written permission of the publishers
Harry N. Abrams, Incorporated, New York
PRINTED AND BOUND IN JAPAN

For
Neil, Gary,
James, Lynn, Scott,
Robert &
Lori

VOLUME
TWO

472 Portrait of Mrs. Samuel Chandler *by Winthrop Chandler, a relative, painted about 1780. The artist was born in Woodstock, Connecticut, in 1747, and was probably apprenticed to a house painter in Boston, where he eked out a living painting signs and doing odd jobs. National Gallery of Art, Washington, D.C. Gift of Edgar William and Bernice Chrysler Garbisch*

BOOK
FOUR

Woman's World

BOOK FOUR: *Woman's World*

1679

1679 *Tending fire, a full-time chore at the giant kitchen fireplace (six feet high, nine feet wide, and four feet deep) of the Governor's Palace in Williamsburg, Virginia. The fireplace could accommodate a number of different foods cooking at one time, but each required individual care. With family, servants, and a constant stream of guests, the kitchen staff often had to prepare meals for sixty or more. "Fifty-two dined with me yesterday," wrote the governor, Lord Botetourt, in 1769, "and I expect that number here today." Over the fireplace hang a variety of utensils including the clockwork-jack timing device, extreme right. Photograph courtesy Colonial Williamsburg* **1680–1683** *Mortars and pestles for grinding grains and spices, turned of hard woods such as maple, walnut, and ash* **1684** *Larder of the manor house of an eighteenth-century southern plantation, displaying meat hooks suspended from ceiling and a large variety of food storage containers including earthenware jugs and crocks, wooden tubs, casks, kegs, and woven baskets. Photograph courtesy Mount Vernon Ladies Association, Mount Vernon, Virginia* **1685** *Washington's kitchen at Mount Vernon with well-equipped fireplace displaying wrought-iron pothooks, spits, firedogs, and utensils. Also in evidence are a number of pewter, copper, and brass items, including the spiral wooden handled warming pan on the left wall. Photograph courtesy Mount Vernon Ladies Association, Mount Vernon, Virginia*

What's Cooking

1680 — 1683

From early wills and inventories one gains a significant view of the Colonial household. Such a list as "1 frying pan, 2 skillets, 3 bake pains, iron pothooks, warming pan and trivet" suggests the austerity of existence in the New World. Family life revolved around the common room, which was usually teeming with all sorts of activity. Here the settler huddled to keep warm, mend his tools, and read his Bible, while his wife wove cloth, made the family's clothing, and cooked.

The common room was termed the hall before it was called the kitchen, especially in New England and the Middle Atlantic states, where winters were severe. A huge fireplace, derived in type from that of an English manor house, was the hub of this room, supplying warmth, light, and a source of heat for all cooking and baking. Built of stone and later of

1684

1685

1686

1687

1688

brick, the fireplace was topped by a broad, rough-hewn lintel ten to twelve feet long, made from a solid tree trunk. At first the lintel was set flush with the masonry wall; later it projected from it, providing a shelf for tools, kitchen utensils, and other artifacts.

As more comfortable houses became possible, the common room ceased to be an all-purpose living area for the family's activities. Beds were removed to separate rooms upstairs; a buttery was created for the churning of butter and the making of buttermilk and cheese; a larder was created for the drying and storage of fruit, vegetables, spices and herbs, and for the hanging of meat and dried fish; and a small room or alcove called the pantry accommodated china, glassware, and stoneware on its shelves. Such specialization developed gradually and depended on a family's economic circumstances. However, the evolution toward comfort and convenience was more rapid in urban areas and on the large plantations of the South, where there was an abundance of domestic help.

In the seventeenth century, cooking at the open fireplace was carried on by three distinct methods: boiling, roasting, and baking, each of which required special utensils. Boiling, and the later refinement of steaming, meant cooking in hot water in a pot or kettle. At first, the Colonist used a lug pole, a wooden bar placed across the fireplace at a distance from the intense heat. Later on, this bar was replaced by an iron crane that was fastened into one side

of the chimney and arranged like a supporting bracket. Pots and kettles were hung on this crane by pothooks, also called trammels. The housewife could swing the crane into the room, hang her pots and kettles on it, then return it to the fire. She was kept very busy, having continually to gauge the heat of the fire and tend it. Roasting consisted of cooking chunks of meat, game, or poultry on the open fire. Here the housewife used a spit; this sharp iron rod, supported on two forked uprights in front of the fire, was thrust into one end of the meat. The handle at one end of the spit required turning, usually done by one of the children. (Later, in the eighteenth century, a mechanical clock arrangement was invented to do the laborious job of turning the roast.) Baking was done with dry heat in a closed compartment. The earliest baking utensil was the heavy, covered pan with legs, called a bake kettle, which was usually placed directly on the red-hot embers. These covered pans came in various sizes and shapes. Other necessary iron cooking utensils included long-handled skillets, cooking pots, tea kettles, gravy-drip broilers, rotary broilers of the gridiron type, trivets, toasters, waffle irons, and plate warmers that hung from one of the andirons.

When chimneys came to be built of brick, a separate oven with a built-in flue and an iron door opening into the kitchen was incorporated in the fireplace. For best results, a hot fire of dry wood, called oven wood, was built about once a week and fed until the bricks

1690

1689

1692

were hot. Wood and ashes were then swept out, the iron door closed, and as many foods as the oven could accommodate, such as baked beans, brown bread, and pies, were pushed in by a special long-handled shovel called a peel.

Kitchen utensils since the arrival of the Pilgrims have been fashioned from wood, stoneware, pewter, tin, iron, copper, and brass. Wood was used extensively for plates (called trenchers), platters, bowls, ladles, and tableware. The wooden pitcher, called a noggin, was passed from mouth to mouth. The tankard, staved and hooped, with a cover, was another wooden drinking vessel. Kept near the fireplace, it held warm toddy and was used for guests rather than for ordinary drinking by the family at the table. The use of a wooden table service, which was easily made on the woodturner's lathe, was a matter of economy with most of the early settlers. Families of wealth adopted china and pewter, relegating this treenware to kitchen use and the servants' quarters. The plentiful supply and variety of wood encouraged the handy householder to shape many items that could be made by turning or simple carpentry. Circular boxes for storage were also used extensively in the kitchen. They were made from thin layers of previously moistened softwoods and pliant birch in many sizes—from pill boxes to spice boxes to those large enough to hold a

wheel of cheese. The mortar and pestle for grinding and crushing grains and spices were usually fashioned from maple, walnut burls, or birch.

The majority of kitchen utensils were made from iron. Wrought iron was used to make tools, prongs, forks, skewers, pothooks, spits, gridirons, toasters, steelyards, firedogs, and trivets. Iron was a common, readily available material mined in many areas from the earliest days of the Colonial period. However, despite their extreme industriousness, the Colonial blacksmiths could not keep pace with the increasing demand for service. Such was the smith's usefulness that he was placed under special guard at the time of the Revolution, since he supplied the tools of war. The characteristics of the Colonial blacksmith's handiwork are utilitarian forms and lack of ornamentation. Old World decorative effects and whorls do not appear in Early American ironwork, and only occasionally does a kitchen artifact incorporate an extraneous curve or scroll. Even the Pennsylvania German smiths, known to favor decoration, practiced restraint and stressed utility. Excavations at Williamsburg, in Virginia—one of the most aristocratic and wealthy of the Colonies—have revealed thousands of iron artifacts, among which are carpenters' tools, carriage hardware, kitchen equipment, and door hinges. Almost without

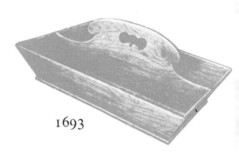

1693

1686–1694 *Kitchen woodenware, or treen, including scoop, 1686; mixing bowl, 1687; butter paddle, 1688; butter scoop or ladle, 1689; spoon,* *1690; cheese board, 1691; bucket, 1692; knife box, 1693; and spoon rack, 1694*

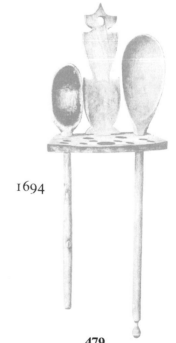

1694

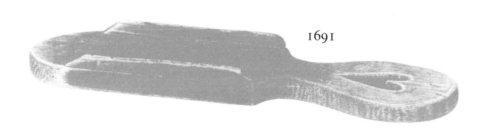

1691

1695

1696

1697

exception—including items found at the site of the Governor's Palace—these are simple and utilitarian in design.

Brass and copper, in widespread use for kitchen utensils, continued to be imported from Europe well into the nineteenth century. However, there were braziers in the Colonies as early as 1717, in New York and Philadelphia. Lighter than iron, copper and brass items dented easily and thus had a shorter life. These metals, which could be shaped from sheets and easily brazed at the joints, were used for tea- and coffeepots, urns, skillets, frying pans, saucepans, washbasins, warming pans, skimmers, ladles, scoops, measures, and scales. In the middle of the eighteenth century, braziers and coppersmiths advertised their wares and repair services in Colonial

1695–1704 *Metal kitchen utensils, including iron skillet, 1695; copper kettles, 1696, 1698; flour sifter, 1697; brass starch strainer, 1699; copper pot for candy making, 1700; copper ladle for candy making, 1701; brass tea kettle, 1702; tin tea kettle, 1703; and copper tea kettle, 1704. Except for 1697 and 1701–1703, c. 1830–65, most utensils are of late eighteenth-century make*

1699

1698

480

1701

journals and, at a later date, in city directories. Frequent references to such services exist in the gazettes of the larger cities. By the end of the century, a number of brass foundries were established, so that cast brass as well as hammered sheet brasswares were available.

Jacob Wilkins, of New York, advertised all manner of brasswork at the "Sign of the Brass Andiron and Candlestick." Peter van Norden operated a brass foundry in Bound Brook, New Jersey, where he manufactured kitchenwares as well as brass andirons, candlesticks, shoe and buckle ornaments, pitchers, measures, pipkins, coal scuttles, and brass kettles "from a barrel to a quart," sold in nests. Brass kettles could be cast, or hammered over a mold with the handles riveted on. A complete kitchen assortment of bright, gleaming brass-

1702

1703

1704

1700

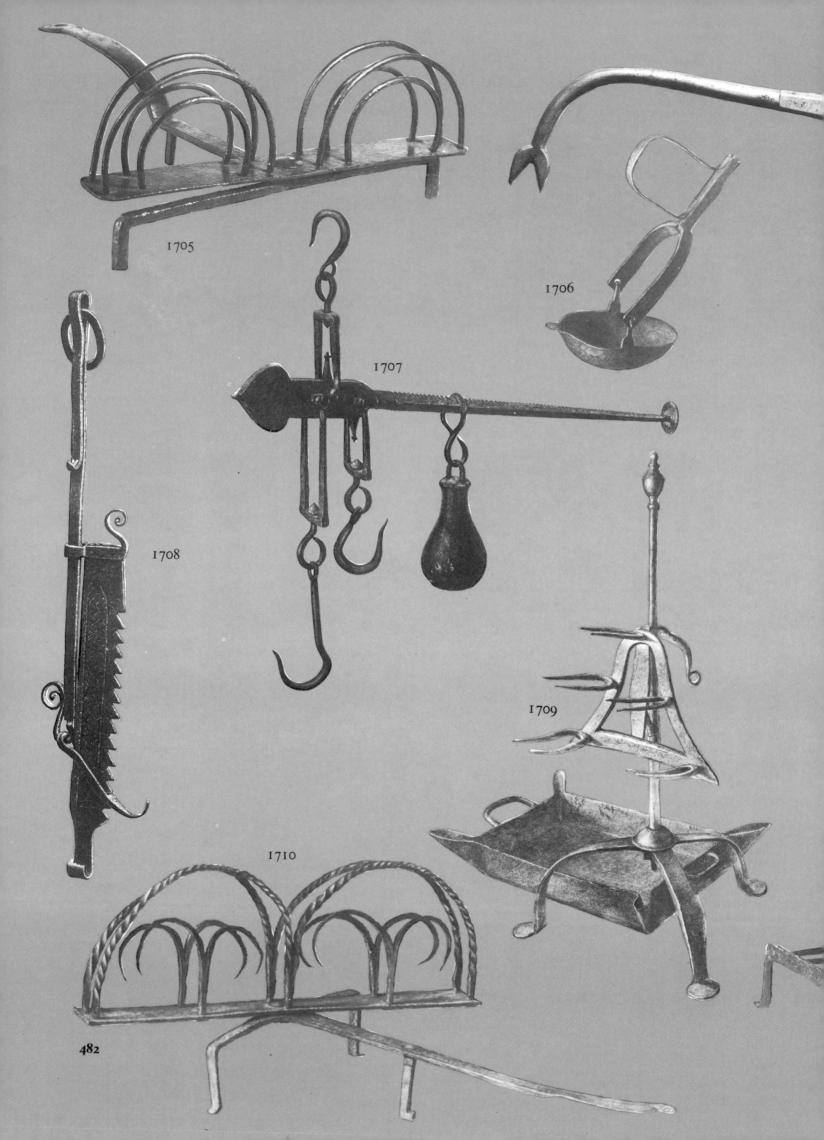

1705

1706

1707

1708

1709

1710

ware was rare—indeed, a sure sign of affluence in early days. Today a collection of these wares may be seen in the kitchen of the Governor's Palace in Williamsburg.

By the nineteenth century, the brass industry centered largely in New England. Important foundries were located in Waterbury, Bridgeport, and Torrington, Connecticut. Copper was used for the same kinds of articles as brass and was ideal for warming pans, kettles, and saucepans. A major objection to the use of copper, however, was its disagreeable taste. To overcome this, a thin coating of tin was used to line the inside of most copper culinary vessels. When this coating wore away, the vessel had to be relined. The bottoms of kettles and pots also needed constant repairing. Like brass, copper utensils could be both hammered and cast. The first hammered utensils were beaten on an iron mold with a wooden mallet. Spouts and handles were riveted on by hand and were sometimes made from copper tubing. Surface decoration was rarely applied to brass or copper utensils, with the exception of warming pans and trivets. The warming pan, used for warming cold bedsheets, had a hinged lid with pierced designs and, often, scrolls or foliated engraving, and the brass tops of trivets had similar designs, following English precedent.

1705–1713 *Wrought-iron kitchen utensils, including toasters, 1705, 1710, 1713; grease lamp, 1706; steelyard, 1707; pothook, 1708; roasting stand and drip pan, 1709; trivet, 1711; and piecrust cutter, 1712* **1714–1717** *Cast-iron kitchen utensils, including skillet, 1714; three-legged pot, 1715; mortar, 1716; and muffin pan, 1717. Figures 1705, 1711, 1712, and 1716 from photographs*

483

1718

1719

1720

1721

484

1722   1723

1718–1726 *Variously called match safes, matchboxes, and match holders, these containers were found in every kitchen as well as in other rooms in the period 1860–1900. Most were made of cast iron, as are those illustrated here, but tin boxes, stamped out of sheet metal and decorated, were also available in a variety of designs in this period*

Overleaf: GALLERY OF KITCHEN UTENSILS AND GADGETS.   *Buckets:* **1730, 1738** *butter churns:* **1737, 1752** *cake molds:* **1736, 1751, 1756** *charcoal burner:* **1776** *cheese strainer:* **1746** *cherry stoner:* **1765** *coffee mills:* **1728, 1758, 1762** *coffee roaster:* **1731** *dish drainer:* **1774** *dough trough,* **1780** *food choppers:* **1734, 1735, 1742, 1755** *ice cream freezer:* **1777** *copper and tin kettles and pots:* **1727, 1739, 1743, 1750, 1763, 1775** *iron kettles and pans:* **1733, 1741, 1749, 1760, 1769** *knife box:* **1747** *ladle:* **1757** *match holders:* **1744, 1748, 1764, 1773** *mortars and pestles:* **1754, 1759, 1768** *rolling pin:* **1767** *scoops:* **1772, 1779** *spoon rack:* **1766** *water kegs:* **1745, 1771** *wrought-iron utensils:* **1732, 1753, 1761, 1770** *toasters:* **1729, 1778**

1724

1725

1726

1727

1728

1729

1730

173

1736

1737

1738

1739

174

1745

1746

1747

1748

174

1754

1755

1756

1757

175

1763

1764

1765

1766

176

1772

1773

1774

1775

1776

1732

1733

1734

1735

1741

1742

1743

1744

1750

1751

1752

1753

1759

1760

1761

1762

1768

1769

1770

1771

1777

1778

1779

1780

1781 *Virginia "shoo-fly" chair, a simple but ingenious device operated by a treadle that activates the cloth strips overhead. Photograph courtesy Colonial Williamsburg* **1782** *Wire beater, operated by rapidly opening and closing the wooden handles*

To Beat a Better Batter

1782

M ost domestic timesaving devices have been invented for use in the kitchen. This was especially true during the Colonial period, when the kitchen was the center of all household activity. The day was never long enough for the housewife, who often had to feed a family of ten or more in addition to farmhands. The day's meals required endless preparation before the actual cooking could begin: cutting, shredding, chopping, beating, grinding, mixing, pitting, and paring. Hence, each new gadget that could afford some relief to the cook was taken up with enthusiasm. As appliances invaded the kitchen in a bewildering variety, the housewife had to adapt to new cooking methods. She had, for example, to adjust to changing heat sources, first from the open hearth to the enclosed firebox and, more recently, to the gas and electric stove. She also had to adjust to copper or brass pots, instead of iron ones.

The steady stream of laborsaving kitchen appliances included eggbeaters, meat grinders, sausage stuffers, kraut cutters, apple parers, cider presses, cherry pitters, and ice-cream freezers. Before these started to appear in the mid-nineteenth century, homemade coffee and spice grinders—miniature imitations of the age-old milling and grinding apparatus—were already found in many kitchens. However, with the popularization of cast iron, coffee grinders with cast-iron wheels and parts began to be manufactured in great numbers.

A distinctly American device was the apple parer, extremely useful since apples were a

1783

household staple for pies, applesauce, apple butter, and cider. The principle of the turning lathe was the basic concept behind every apple-peeling and coring gadget. As early as 1803, a wooden appliance with a fork for holding the apple, a handle and turning device, and a sharp knife edge was the forerunner of similar machines which developed throughout the century. At harvest time, it was not uncommon for a single household to pare three hundred bushels of apples for use throughout the winter months. This need led to the addition of apple-paring bees to the existing quilting bees and barn-raising celebrations, all festive occasions at which gallons of cider, America's most popular drink, were consumed.

Eggbeaters represented a new application of the principle of the hand drill. Through an arrangement of gears that operated revolving wire beaters, the manual beating process was accelerated. Another useful mechanical device was one for chopping and mincing which, by a continuous up-and-down movement of a blade, cut and shredded meats and vegetables in an efficient manner similar to the operation of a guillotine.

The many thousands of patents issued for household devices evidence human ingenuity and confirm the fact that mechanization in the home, as typified by these kitchen aids, is an activity for which Americans have been largely responsible. Some of these early appliances were cumbersome in construction, but many were simple and forthright, possessing an inherent beauty by virtue of honest lines and forms. However, in the mid-nineteenth century, when cast iron became the material commonly used for many household items, manufacturers began to decorate these appliances with elaborate designs. In so doing they expressed the Victorian desire to disguise utilitarian purpose, preferring to create objects which were believed to be aesthetic additions to the home.

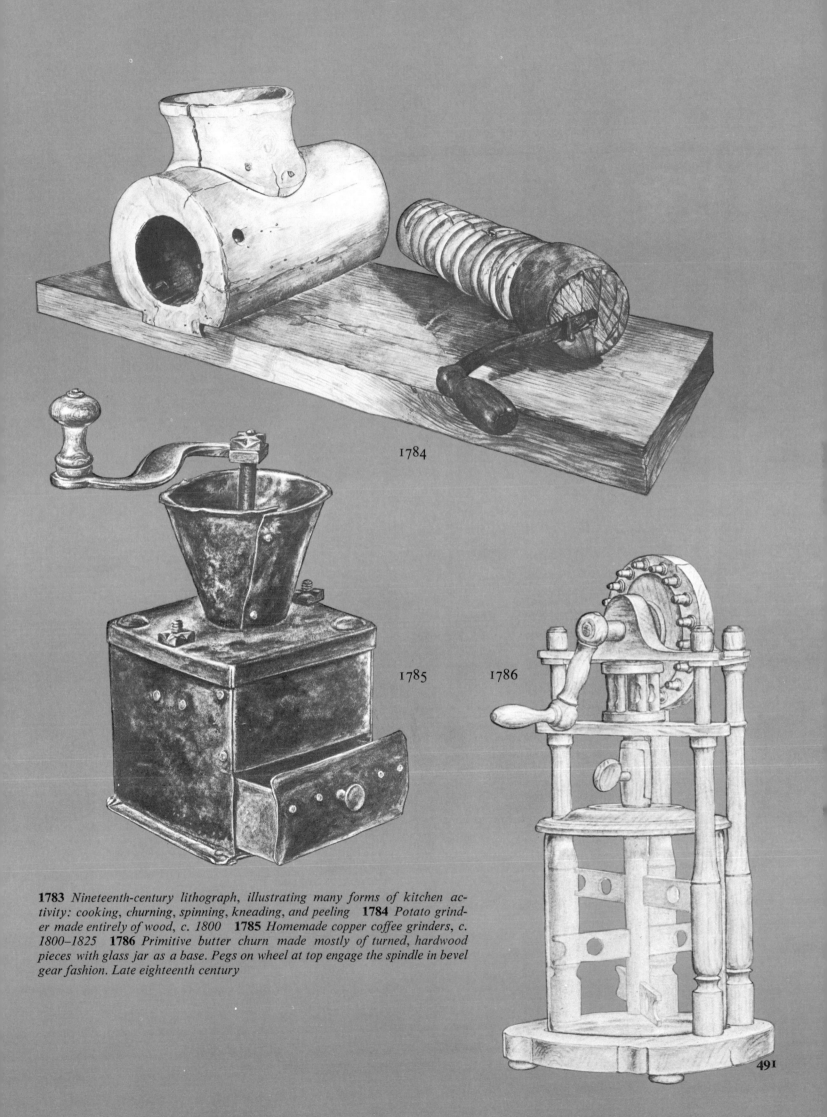

1784

1785   1786

1783 *Nineteenth-century lithograph, illustrating many forms of kitchen activity: cooking, churning, spinning, kneading, and peeling* **1784** *Potato grinder made entirely of wood, c. 1800* **1785** *Homemade copper coffee grinders, c. 1800–1825* **1786** *Primitive butter churn made mostly of turned, hardwood pieces with glass jar as a base. Pegs on wheel at top engage the spindle in bevel gear fashion. Late eighteenth century*

1787   1788

1789

492

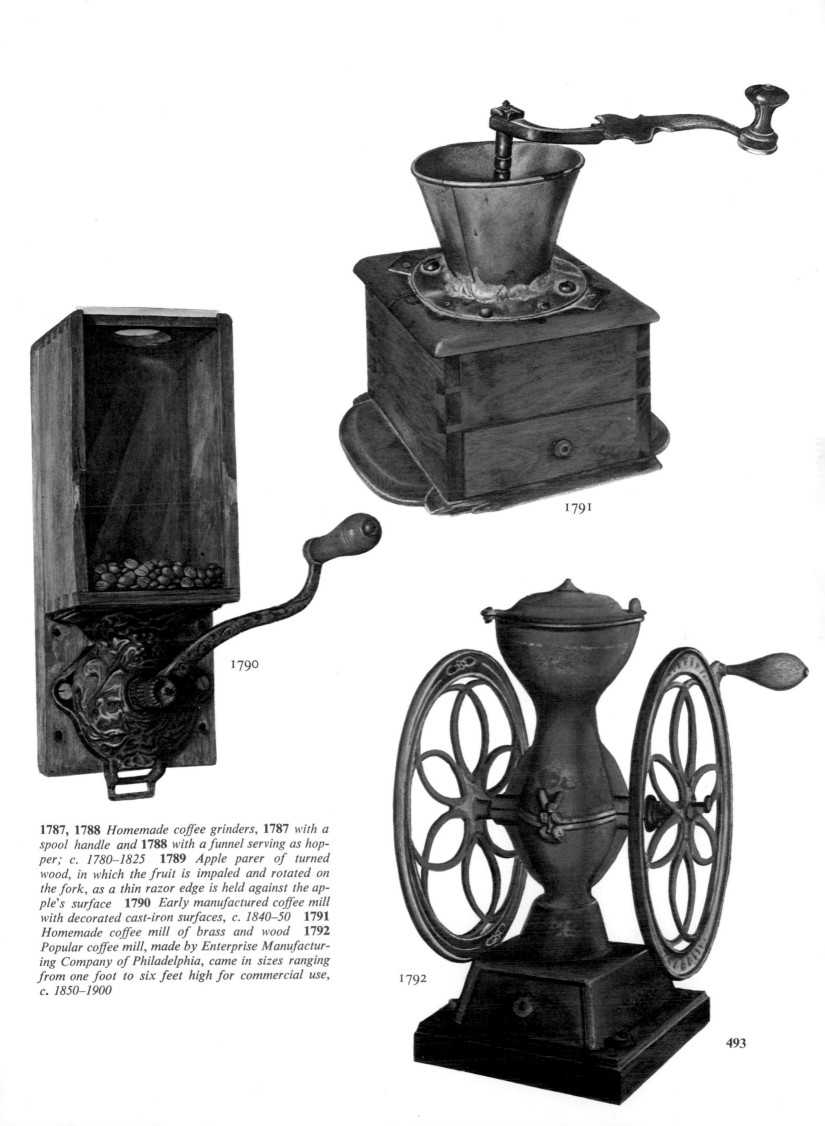

1790

1791

1792

1787, 1788 *Homemade coffee grinders,* **1787** *with a spool handle and* **1788** *with a funnel serving as hopper; c. 1780–1825* **1789** *Apple parer of turned wood, in which the fruit is impaled and rotated on the fork, as a thin razor edge is held against the apple's surface* **1790** *Early manufactured coffee mill with decorated cast-iron surfaces, c. 1840–50* **1791** *Homemade coffee mill of brass and wood* **1792** *Popular coffee mill, made by Enterprise Manufacturing Company of Philadelphia, came in sizes ranging from one foot to six feet high for commercial use, c. 1850–1900*

493

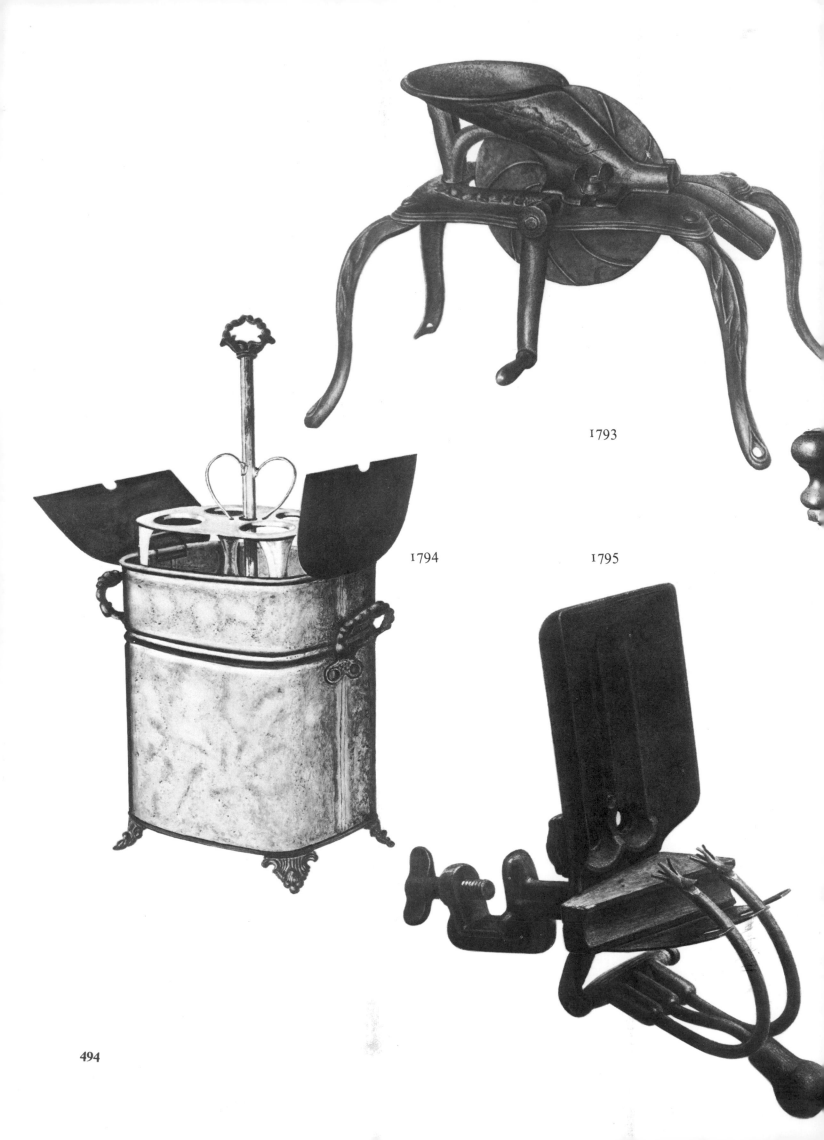

1793

1794

1795

1793 *Cast-iron cherry pitter, with legs resembling furniture supports, decorated with acanthus foliage, c. 1860* **1794** *Tin egg boiler with cast-iron legs* **1795** *Cherry pitter designed to fasten over table edge* **1796** *Box-type coffee grinder, popular because the operator could sit on a chair and hold it between the knees while grinding. Delicately ornamented cast-iron parts date this mill, c. 1850–80* **1797** *Homemade, wall-type coffee mill, requiring user to hold a vessel underneath to catch the ground beans. Made in Louisiana in 1846* **1798** *Dog-shaped cast-iron nut cracker, c. 1860–80*

1796

1797

1798

1799

A Trivet for the Hot Pot

1800

1801

THE TRIVET WAS FIRST introduced into the Colonies from England in the seventeenth century. It was a three-legged or occasionally a four-legged stand for resting pots or kettles and stood on the stone hearth. It was made of wrought iron, but its flat top was a piece of highly polished brass, in a pierced design. The earliest forms used the owner's initials, often worked into attractive motifs in the current Stuart, Chippendale, or Georgian styles. The trivet was sometimes called a spider because "spiders," or frying pans, were also three-legged. Fireside trivets were made with a turned wooden handle, as well as hooks on the forward end, so that they could be hung on a fire bar when not in use. The use of brass for the top plate gradually disappeared, and the entire form was fashioned from wrought iron by the local blacksmith. At times the shape was crude, but later examples show a variety of forms and decorated bases. The tall

1799 *Flatiron stand or trivet with design representing exuberant Victorian taste, incorporating a vase out of which grows a tree of life, scrolls, and floral and foliate forms. Latter half of the nineteenth century* 1800 *Maple-handled, high-legged trivet showing English influence. Brass top with compass motif is supported by wrought-iron legs, c. 1775–90* 1801 *Flatiron holder with design showing an eagle poised atop a heart within a circlet of laurel leaves. Made in the Zoarite Community, Zoar, Ohio, mid-nineteenth century*

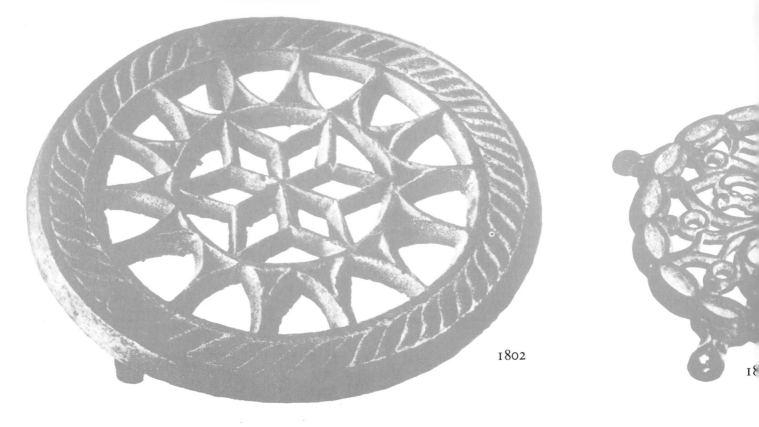

1802

18

legs eventually gave way to short ones no more than an inch or two in height.

The three-legged construction influenced the overall design, for in its simplest form the trivet was a triangle with a handle at the blunt end. However, the smith had an opportunity to exhibit his ingenuity when he shaped and formed the metal in its molten state. The feet and handle were affixed when the body shape was completed, unless, of course, the handle was an extension of the base.

Another related form produced by the smith for kitchen use was the gridiron, a circular footed shape, the top, flat surface of which was marked by parallel bars or by honeycomb, wavy, or serpentine crosspieces in various arrangements. The revolving grill

pivoted around a center pin so that it could be turned easily when used for broiling meat. Wrought-iron trivets and gridirons were made throughout the Colonies during the seventeenth and eighteenth centuries. Those produced in Pennsylvania were heart-shaped or incorporated hearts, fylfots, or common barn symbols in their designs.

Iron stands for flatirons were also called trivets, and were made for use on a ledge, shelf, or ironing board. Like the trivet, they were usually three-cornered to accommodate the similarly shaped flatiron. With the development of foundries, both flatirons and

1805

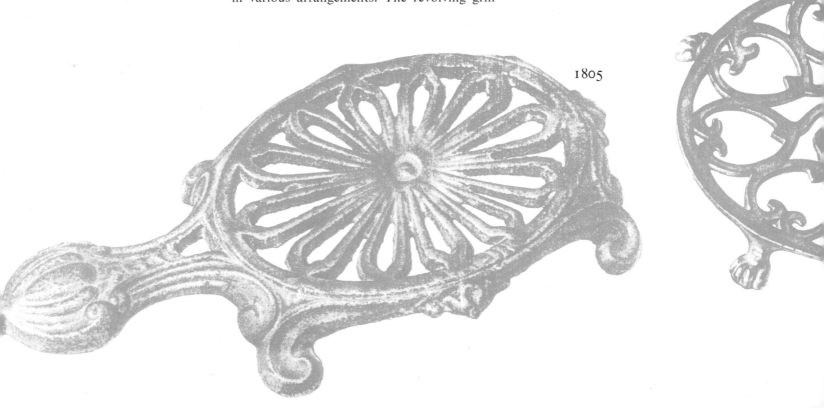

1804

trivets were made in a great variety of designs. This trend began about 1830, and by 1850 trivets of cast iron had almost completely replaced their wrought-iron predecessors. Instead of being crafted by a blacksmith who had been the designer as well as the maker, the newer cast-iron products resulted from a partnership of patternmaker and foundryman. While earlier cast-iron trivets had featured hearts, eagles, stars, and scrolls, as well as such patriotic motifs as George Washington and Miss Liberty, after 1850 the designs became more involved, expressing the prevailing Victorian taste for ornate forms. Naturalistic leaves and flowers, grapes, pineapples, cherubs, and lovebirds were common motifs, as somewhat later in the century were manufacturers' initials and company marks. Borders incorporating mottoes also came into vogue and included popular sayings such as "Good Luck," "Purity, Truth, and Love," and such trade phrases as "Best on Earth."

1802–1807 *Circular-shaped flatiron holders, with or without handles, were found more versatile than the three-footed trivet because there was less chance of their tipping over. Geometrical designs, generally centering around stars, sunbursts, or open centers, predominated*

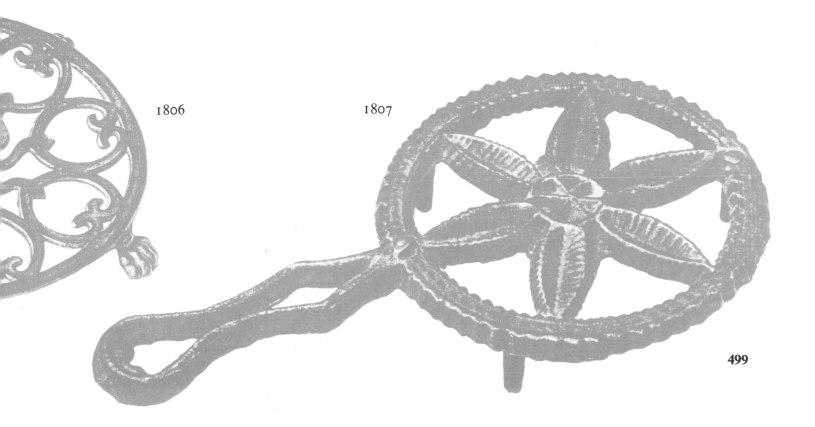

1806   1807

1808

1809

1810

500

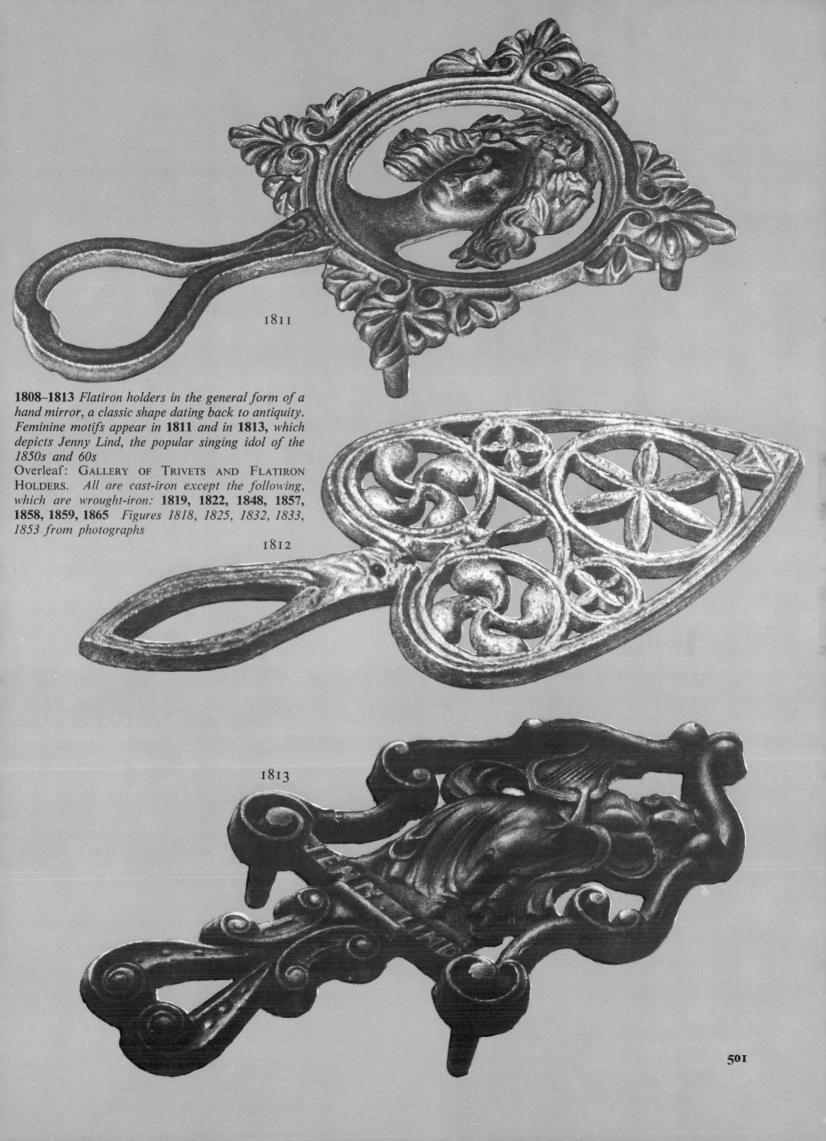

1811

1808–1813 *Flatiron holders in the general form of a hand mirror, a classic shape dating back to antiquity. Feminine motifs appear in* **1811** *and in* **1813**, *which depicts Jenny Lind, the popular singing idol of the 1850s and 60s*

Overleaf: GALLERY OF TRIVETS AND FLATIRON HOLDERS. *All are cast-iron except the following, which are wrought-iron:* **1819, 1822, 1848, 1857, 1858, 1859, 1865** *Figures 1818, 1825, 1832, 1833, 1853 from photographs*

1812

1813

1814

1815

1816

1817

1818

1823

1824

1825

1826

1832

1833

1834

1835

1840

1841

1842

1843

1849

1850

1851

1852

1858

1859

1860

1819

1820

1821

1822

1828

1829

1830

1831

1836

1837

1838

1839

1844

1845

1846

1847

1848

1854

1855

1856

1857

1862

1863

1864

1865

1866

1867

1867 *A well-equipped Colonial kitchen stocked a variety of cake and cookie boards, vigorously carved of maple, walnut, and oak for hard wear and to withstand the oven's heat. Many of these can be seen on the shelf above the brick oven. Photograph courtesy Colonial Williamsburg* **1868** *Maple butter mold, with strawberry design* **1869** *Walnut cookie board, with realistically carved fruit, floral, and crown motifs, used for molding holiday sweets similar to marzipan cakes and springerle. Made in Ohio by Swiss immigrants*

Cake Boards, Cookie & Butter Molds

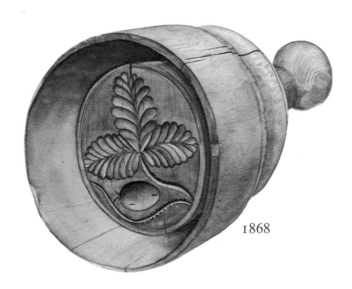

1868

1869

IF A PRESENT-DAY housewife decided to decorate her supply of butter with an interesting design, she would probably be accused of "gilding the lily." A few generations ago, however, when every rural family did its own churning, butter was seldom served unadorned; it was taken to the table in the form of animals, birds, tulips, or hearts, "just for fancy," as the Pennsylvania Germans expressed it.

This custom of embellishing everyday products has been observed in many countries from early times. From the decoration of food containers, it was a short step to decorating the food itself. The simplest means of creating a decorative design was by impressing it with a stamp or shaping it in a mold. The custom of decorative molds for butter was of Continental origin, particularly practiced by the farmers and peasants of Scandinavia, Switzerland, Germany, and the Alsace region. When this tradition was practiced in the Colonies, the butter was referred to as "print" butter, a term still in use although as a general practice this charming custom has long since been abandoned.

Unfortunately, there is scant record of the use and design of butter molds. They were considered artifacts of lowly origin and as such were very much taken for granted—as was the case with most of the simple artifacts from the early Colonial period. Thus there was no conception that they had value as objects of art. What little information exists is the result of piecing together acquired facts with observations of the objects themselves,

1870

1871

based on a close examination of their carving characteristics. Since the molds were the work of untutored whittlers who practiced a simple technique called "chip carving," this art was limited to simple cuts and twists executed quickly with a sharp knife. Most butter molds were either of pine or poplar, as these were easily carved; however, cherry, maple, and walnut were also used. The earliest extant butter molds were made between 1775 and 1825 and were carved from native woods found in Pennsylvania, New York, and the New England states. The molds show crudely whittled designs in disks about three inches in diameter that are reminiscent of European patterns and hex symbols. At first the molds did not have handles; later, crude handles were inserted into the disks.

Regional traits manifest themselves not so much in carving technique as in motifs. British motifs appear in the New England molds, while the influence of the southern European Palatinate is apparent in the Pennsylvania German ones. British butter molds, although more symmetrical and formal than those of New England, incorporated naturalistic forms, carefully spaced on the face of a mold, and were bordered with various well-defined patterns. The British carvings seem closely related to the designs of contemporary cabinetmakers. British designs included strawberry plants, fruits, and flowers and revealed the mark of a professional wood-carver, not the hand of a farmer who decorated his molds spontaneously, as was the case with the New England molds. Foliate motifs, with curving lines and asymmetrical patterning, imbue the New England molds with an unsophisticated charm. They are the product of artisans familiar with birds, animals, trees, and fruit, whose art experience was limited but whose design sense in this folk-art form was great.

A tradition of fine craftsmanship is evident in the work fashioned by the immigrants from the Palatinate, who settled along the Delaware River and in the regions to the west. Their work displays an admirable knowledge of wood carving and expresses a vigorous simplicity. Comparatively few motifs were employed; these included the conventionalized tulip; the heart and star, which appear in nearly all their decorations; and sheaves of wheat, acorns, and crescents. Frequently the pineapple, a symbol of hospitality, was used.

Since the eagle appeared as a popular decorative motif during the Federal period, it is not surprising that it is found in many forms on butter molds. The cow with milk-filled udder standing serenely under a tree and beautiful elaborations of the hex mark, a symbol of protection, are also frequent motifs. Skilled and versatile carvers wrought a great variety of design versions of each motif. Often graceful leaf forms filled empty spaces and herringbone patterns made other areas more interesting. The outer borders of the butter molds were contained within notched or striated edges.

In the marketplace the butter producer was identified by his design, which thus took on a trademark value. The superstitious farmer took every precaution to maintain the quality of his product, including placing a horseshoe over his springhouse door or a huge hex mark on his barn. One enterprising buttery introduced a note of advertising by adding the

1870–1872 *Cookie cutters, fashioned of tin ribbons and then soldered to a flat base, were designed in many forms. Illustrated are the American eagle, a deer, and a horse and rider. Pennsylvania German, nineteenth century* **1873** *The pie cupboard or "safe," a ventilated wooden cupboard with perforated tin doors, was used to store pies and cakes, protecting them from marauding children before mealtime. Made in Pennsylvania*

1872

1873

507

1874

1875

1876

words "Good butter . . . Taste it" to its moldmark.

Butter molds were either cup-shaped or boxed. When cup-shaped, the decoration was placed on the bottom of a plunger used to eject the butter. The butter mold was dipped in scalding, then in cold, water before the butter was packed into it. One unusual mold opened in the form of a Maltese cross with a different design on each of the five hinged sides. Molds were made in various sizes: pounds, halves, quarters, and eighths, although some, probably at a later date, were made to produce individual pats for table use. The designs on both stamps and molds were usually incised so that a raised impression resulted, although there are a few instances of a carved design which resulted in an intaglio impression.

It is rare to discover a field of fundamental design as rich and fertile as that represented by these molds, which until quite recently were overlooked by collectors of Americana. The recognition of their importance as a folk art demonstrates how neglected arts frequently have much to offer students of design and those interested in national traditions.

1874 *Semicircular butter mold with palmette motif* **1875** *Cake boards of a European type known as springerle molds. Varied subjects and precise detailing with razor-like tools reveal domestic details as well as love of farm animals. Made in Pennsylvania, c. 1835* **1876** *Walnut springerle board in which the twenty squares constitute a nursery catalogue of familiar forms and figures, c. 1805–25*

1878   1879

1877 *Love of birds, expressed in twelve squares depicting the hen, rooster, owl, ostrich, duck, swan, grouse, pheasant, and others, Pennsylvania German, 1843. Photograph* **1878** *Raised tin cookie form, featuring farm and folktale subjects. Nineteenth century. Photograph* **1879** *Maple-sugar mold with semi-abstract carved floral forms*

1880

1881

1882

1883   1884

1885

1886

1887

1888

1889

1890

1880–1890 *Poplar, oak, and maple butter molds representing folk art at its best. "Print" butter displayed the maker's mark, to distinguish it from butter marketed in tubs or crocks and brought higher prices. Eagles and other fowl and barnyard animals were popular motifs. These mostly Pennsylvania German make, except for molding box,* **1888,** *from Wisconsin, c. 1880*

1891

1892

1891–1898 *Pennsylvania German butter molds, revealing individuality in choice of motif—the tulip being predominant—and a confident chip-carving technique. Parallel cuts and nicks added interest to the leaf forms; cross-hatching, as in 1893, produced a patterned surface. Striated cuts to resemble feathery forms contribute to the liveliness of the eagle in 1894. The "hex" sign, a common symbol in the region, appears in 1895* **1899–1905** *Butter molds employing leaf and plant forms, especially the tulip, pineapple, and wheat sheaf, demonstrating strong influence of early settlers from Switzerland—a country of butter makers and woodcarvers. Pennsylvania German, first half of nineteenth century. Photograph*

1893

1894

1895

1896

1897

1898

1899 — 1905

515

1906

1907

1908

1909

1906 *Cast-iron cake or cookie form. Photograph* **1907, 1908** *Semicircular butter molds, one featuring the wheat sheaf, and the other the strawberry* **1909** *Acorn motif combined with striated leaf forms. Photograph* **1910–1913** *Abstract leaf forms with serrated edges and V-cut grooves, designs dictated by the cutting tool*

OVERLEAF: GALLERY OF BUTTER MOLDS *Abstract and hex symbols:* **1916, 1920, 1925, 1931, 1932, 1936;** *acorn:* **1914;** *animals and birds:* **1924, 1927;** *eagles:* **1915, 1918, 1922, 1929, 1933;** *plant forms (including tulip and other flowers),* **1917, 1919, 1921, 1923, 1926, 1928, 1930, 1934, 1935, 1937.** *Figures 1914, 1916–1918, 1920–1923, 1925, 1929, 1933, 1936 from photographs*

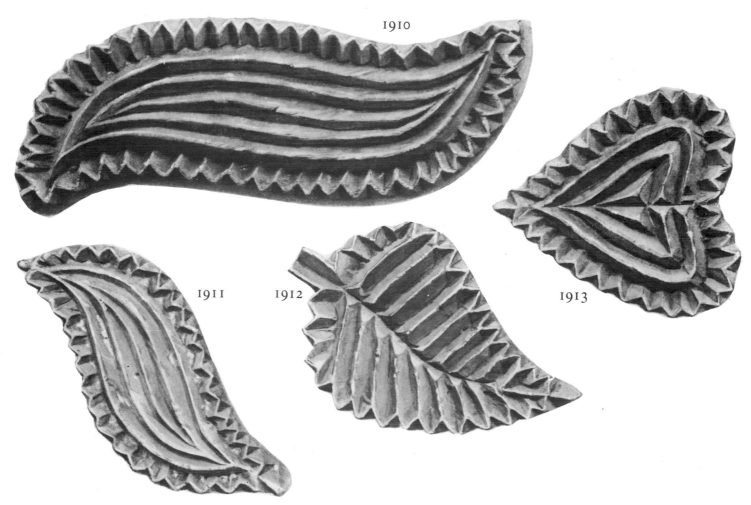

1910

1911   1912   1913

1914

1915

1916

1920

1921

1922

1926

1927

1928

1932

1933

1934

1917

1918

1919

1923

1924

1925

1929

1930

1931

1935

1936

1937

519

Bandboxes for Milady's Bonnets

1939

PAPER-COVERED BANDBOXES for ladies and hatboxes for men were lightweight traveling adjuncts that have no exact equivalent today. On the Continent, during the eighteenth century, bandboxes were used to transport and store elaborately starched ruffs and other personal finery. When the ruff lost its appeal and was replaced with the soft lace collar, the bandbox remained a popular and convenient repository. Ladies found it ideal for storing and transporting jewelry, ribbons, artificial flowers, hairpieces, and a myriad of bagatelles. These early boxes were so delicately constructed and fragile that it is surprising that any have survived the century and a half since they were first fashionable in the United States. However, when yesteryear's travelers boarded coaches for perilous overland journeys, they clung tenaciously to their bandboxes, not entrusting them to coachmen; this habit and the fact that many of them were stored in dry attics may account for their survival.

The American bandbox boom started dur-

1938 *Array of bandboxes stacked in a bandbox room, a common adjunct to a millinery shop in cities and large towns during the second quarter of the nineteenth century. Photograph by Einmars J. Mengis, courtesy Shelburne Museum, Shelburne, Vermont* **1939** *Octagonal bandbox, more costly than oval or circular boxes, since the corners had to be especially reinforced*

1940

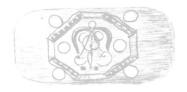

1941

1942

522

ing the second quarter of the nineteenth century, paralleling the development of new means of travel. However, the earliest colored papers for these boxes were probably imported, most of the finely decorated ones coming from France and England. When the box fad gained momentum, the domestic paper printer, using woodblocks, began to design gay and boldly colored papers rather than waiting for the latest imported designs. The earliest use of wallpaper-covered boxes is noted in an advertisement of 1789 by John Fisher of Baltimore, and a fragment of paper from a bandbox owned by Abigail Adams is preserved in the Cooper-Hewitt Museum in New York, noted for its large bandbox collection.

The 1830s and '40s witnessed a steady growth of industrial employment, with women being accepted into the labor force for the first time. This was especially true in New England mill towns, and there was a marked upswing in purchasing power. Girls who had previously not earned anything were now earning two or three dollars per week and thus had the power to purchase such luxury items as bandboxes, which sold for twenty-five or fifty cents each. An enterprising Yankee named Hannah Davis, of Jaffrey, New Hampshire, built a sizable business specializing in the production of bandboxes to cater to this new demand. She started her venture by exchanging boxes for goods and services, but before long it had mushroomed. In order to market large quantities of boxes, she hired a horse and wagon and journeyed to the busy

textile towns where the female labor force would buy her out on the spot. For proof of Hannah Davis's business acumen one had only to watch the factory girls as they left the mill towns for their visits home, "riding on the tops of the old stagecoaches . . . with Aunt Hannah's bandboxes around them like satellites around a sun."

With the opening of the Erie Canal in 1825, linking Buffalo and the Great Lakes to the Hudson River and the Atlantic, a great new territory was serviced by canal and river traffic; and only a few years later, in the early thirties, the first iron rails were being laid in various parts of the East. With the availability of these new avenues of transportation, it was not long before many Americans developed a restless desire to travel. American middle-class society decided it was time to visit its historical shrines, to pay homage to patriotic heroes, and to absorb a bit of culture. Hotels and wayside hostelries catering to the new breed of footloose Americans en route to Niagara Falls, Saratoga Springs, the White Mountains, and other well-advertised spots made the journey more enjoyable. Whatever the method of conveyance, leather luggage, carpetbags, and an array of bandboxes were always in evidence, and the bandbox became the symbol of traveling America.

Although some of these boxes were constructed of thin, bent wood, the majority were made of pasteboard, covered with printed designs and lined with newspapers, thus providing an accurate date of manufacture. The

1943

designs were printed from woodblocks, with inks in three or more colors, in the manner of Japanese prints, though more crudely rendered. There was little need, however, for fineness in detailing or fine registry in color printing, since color and gaiety were all that were needed to attract the buyer's eye. The subject matter selected for the coverings varied greatly from floral and geometric patterns to mythological, Classical, historical, and topical scenes. From studying these designs, one gains an excellent insight into social history, for the modes, manners, and events that characterized American taste and temperament are reflected in the decoration of the bandbox.

Prominent design motifs were scenes commemorating historical events. New York's City Hall, Castle Garden, and Merchant's Exchange, as well as hotels and other institutions, were also featured. National figures, including George Washington, William Harrison, Andrew Jackson, and Zachary Taylor, appeared in gay designs. Many fascinating designs give us a picture of what travel was like: by canal boat amid lively country settings; by fully rigged sailing ship, or the newer steamship *Great Western*; by paddlewheel riverboat; by stagecoach at tavern stops; via "The Windmill Railroad"; and via Clayton's Balloon Ascension. Nothing could be more prophetic than an 1840s' design called "A Peep at the Moon," providing a nineteenth-century version of human efforts in outer space.

Romantic and Neoclassical designs ran the gamut and included gardens of love, lute players, Turkish harem scenes, baskets of flowers, garlands of fruit, the four seasons, castles in Spain, children's games, and rural chores. Birds, beasts, and sea serpents supplied a large number of design motifs, with many of the beasts so freely rendered as to defy description. Scenes of the hunt, which included stags at bay, game warden and poacher, lunch in the fields, and the end of the hunt, were perennial favorites. By far the greatest number of motifs were floral and naturalistic. These were derived from contemporary wallpaper patterns and did not require special tailoring. It was merely necessary to cut enough paper to fit around the box and to select appropriate portions for use on the top.

1944

Most bandbox factories were located in the larger cities. New York, Philadelphia, Boston, and Hartford boasted about thirty of these plants. However, the vogue for bandboxes did not last, and most of these factories were out of business by mid-century. The passing of the stagecoach era and the growth in travel by boat and train called for stouter luggage. Hatboxes which could hold half a dozen hats were made of heavier fabric and reinforced construction, and leather luggage, which could better withstand rough handling at depots, was preferred. Thus the bandbox, which had seen its best days, gradually faded into oblivion.

1945

1946

1940 *Hand-painted Pennsylvania German bride-box of thin spruce, bent to shape around a pine base* **1941** *Pennsylvania bandbox with fruit and leaf motifs, early nineteenth century* **1942** *Bandboxes were invariably lined with newspapers, thus enabling us to date them if no date appears on the box* **1943** *Gentleman's hatbox covered with printed design, c. 1830–40* **1944** *Floral-print wallpaper used for box covering* **1945** *Wallpaper for box covering, featuring a chariot drawn by griffons, c. 1830* **1946** *Box paper with rural scene including church, homes, and birds, c. 1830–40* **1947** *Box paper displays Fire Engine Number 13 in action. Printed in Philadelphia, c. 1831–36*

1947

1948

1949

1950

1951

1952

1953

1954

1955

1948–1958 *Paper coverings for bandboxes were either all-over patterns, usually floral, or scenic designs, in which case the motif was tailored to fit around the box. The former were more easily adapted to the box surface, being used for both sides and top with only the addition of an edging on the lid. Scenic designs were printed on a long strip of paper from wooden blocks and then glued on, with the seam at the back. Typical scenic designs include: "Windmill Railroad," 1949, commemorating the advent of the railroad (c. 1830); scenes of rural life, 1950 (c. 1830), and 1957 (c. 1835); 1956, log cabin with riverboat and sunburst (c. 1840); and 1958, a handsome public building, here an asylum for the deaf and dumb*

Overleaf: GALLERY OF BANDBOXES. *Designs of Classical or mythological origin:* 1961, 1970, 1970; *transportation scenes:* 1960, 1968, 1973; *eagle:* 1967; *floral and decorative:* 1959, 1976, 1978; *historical:* 1963, 1975; *pastoral:* 1962, 1964, 1965, 1969, 1971, 1974, 1977; *scenic:* 1966

1956

1957

1958   **525**

1959

1960

1961

1964

1965

1966

1969

1970

1971

526   1974

1975

1976

1962

1963

1967

1968

1972

1973

1977

1978   527

Hand-hooked for the Home

1980

Making rugs from scraps, strings, and bits of wool and yarn woven together according to personal taste was one of the crafts allocated to the household. The rugs showed the creative instinct of the cottage dweller, and for the long hours of painstaking detail there was a noble satisfaction when the final stitches were put in place.

Experts seem to agree that the art of hooking rugs is an American development, originating in the northeastern section of New England and in the neighboring maritime provinces of Canada. It was brought to these shores by the Scandinavians. The French, English, Welsh, and Scots adopted it during the latter part of the eighteenth century. A long period of gestation occurred; few examples appeared much before 1820. The technique of hooking may be traced to the old method of "thrumming," that is, "of fastening thrums, short cut-off pieces of yarn or cloth, to a background of fabric so as to give a heavy nap. This was usually accomplished by poking the thrums through holes or mesh, so that the two ends showed on one side." The background material was either homespun linen, factory-woven cotton, or burlap. Cloth strips were cut from leftover woolens or scraps, and a metal hook was used to draw the strips through the background fabric into loops. The loops were either cut or left uncut and their length determined

1979 *Universally acknowledged to be one of the rarest of all early American handmade carpets, the famous Caswell rug at the Metropolitan Museum of Art in New York City is an object lesson in native handcrafts. It was made in Castleton, Vermont, in 1835 by Zeruah Higley Guernsey and became known as the "Caswell Carpet" because of her subsequent marriage to Mr. Caswell in 1846. Often referred to as the "Blue Cat Rug" because of a whimsical book about it, it is made up of numerous squares embroidered in what was called "double Kensington stitch," on firm homespun. Its floral motifs, birds and cats, fruits and foliage reveal an exuberant spirit. The portion shown here represents about a quarter of the rug; some two years were spent in the making, from shearing the wool to the dyeing and final embroidery. Its design is a treasure trove of homely inspiration in the best native tradition of needlecraft* **1980** *The bridal couple, only one of almost eighty squares, is a complete, self-contained gem in the Caswell carpet, one of many*

the softness of the pile.

Early hooked rugs show an engaging naiveté of design. With no academic art training, rugmakers ventured into a field involving artistic decisions. The rug area became a canvas on which design, form, color, and texture were combined with skillful needlework to produce a picture. The designer was called on to exercise taste at every turn, a test of blending artistry with manual dexterity.

In the making of hooked rugs, the housewife could select from an abundant range of subject matter. Animals, birds, and buildings required a sense of proportion and scale; geometric and floral designs did not present such problems and thus dominated rug decoration. In the 1850s a rapidly growing interest in rugmaking developed. This became so intense in the East that an enterprising Yankee named E. S. Frost saw vast commercial possibilities in supplying designs.

Frost, a returning Union soldier who had been wounded in the war, was forced to assume an outdoor life for reasons of health. Working as a tin peddler, he soon noticed that his patrons on farms and in New England villages were busily making hooked rugs for their homes. They asked for rug designs, which he and his wife supplied from their own handiwork. Frost shrewdly reasoned that the production of such designs by stenciling could lead to greater sales. His ingenuity was evident from the start: in order to produce a stencil he flattened an old copper boiler and fashioned his stencil outlines with a cold chisel and file, and then printed the design on burlap. His contribution to the hooking of rugs was in the making of patterns, many of which became available to workers throughout the country. He popularized a rural art form for which women of all areas had long shown an aptitude. Whereas Frost's designs were welcomed by many women, mass-production unfortunately robbed them of originality, spontaneity, and individual interpretation.

The art was carried a step further along commercial lines when the demand for wool strips led to their production by factory methods. The frugal housewife no longer had

to salvage cast-off garments and patiently shred them into usable strips. If anything, the ease with which one could purchase woolen strips helped speed the making of more rugs by more housewives.

The life of a hooked rug is short; its longevity depends on the base through which the strands are pulled. Antique rugs were hooked into a background of linen or hemp sacking, stronger than jute or burlap. The linen or hemp was then stretched on a tambour, or wooden frame, and the pattern marked with ink or charcoal. Rugs which covered the floor were necessarily short-lived; others designed as bedspreads were subjected to less wear. Several prominent museum pieces of this type date from the late eighteenth century.

In rugmaking the designs and patterns may run the gamut from the abstract and geometric, and the floral and naturalistic, to the pictorial and illustrative, such as scenic, historical, and patriotic bits of Americana. In the first category there are basketweaves, blocks, frets, wavy lines, zigzags, and the guilloche (interlaced bands, the openings of which are filled with round ornaments). Variants and combinations of these—in color, design, and juxtaposition—depended on the designer's versatility. Where the accumulation of cloth remnants did not permit the matching of colors, the crazy-quilt approach gave free rein to the creator's imagination. Mosaic work, inch squares, and the popular quilt motifs offered a wide choice of patterns, depending on shading and color variations. Geometric shapes—circle, square, triangle, diamond, and star—presented numerous possibilities.

Floral motifs, in formal or informal arrangements, loose sprays, garlands, and festoons used as either central medallions or border offered almost unlimited potential for originality. The floral bouquet has been the dominant design theme of thousands of hooked rugs, and the free interpretation of the floral forms often resulted in young, fresh designs. Many hundred-year-old hooked rugs look as if they have just emerged from the studios or workshops of today's avant-garde artists.

1981

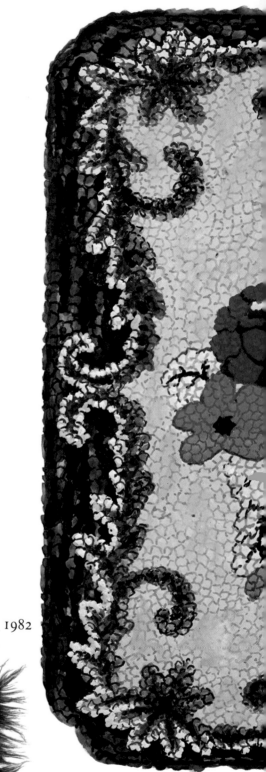

1982

1983

1981–1985 *Florals are favorites. The universal appeal of flowers, their profusion of color, and the ease with which they can be drawn and hooked account for floral popularity in the design of hooked rugs. The more successful rugs involve a schematic plan such as those in which an outer arrangement forms a border, as in* **1982** *and* **1985,** *or a series of concentric ovals, as in* **1981**

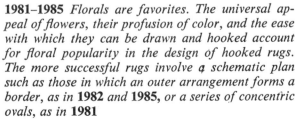

1986

1988

1987

 1989

1990

1986 *A central bouquet of flowers is surrounded by a floral ring, further echoed in the corner treatment* **1987** *Realism gives way to more abstract rendering* **1988** *The large symmetrical brackets of floral forms, quite modern in their free shapes, make an enclosure for simplified forms within* **1989** *The peasant or homespun quality of these floral and leaf forms makes for an attractive composition* **1990** *The four corner leaf forms are magnified to large proportions and symmetrically arranged for greatest impact, while the center unit is reduced to a subservient role*

1991

1992

536

1993

1994

1991 *In the field of geometric design the simplest motif involves a series of small squares repeated with variations in color treatment* **1992** *A combination of straight-line borders, cut corners, and oval centerpiece* **1993** *An original scroll design in which opposite curves from a floral center create counterbalance* **1994** *Borders of straight lines and corner pieces contrast with a scalloped enclosure*

1995

1996

1997

538

1998

1999

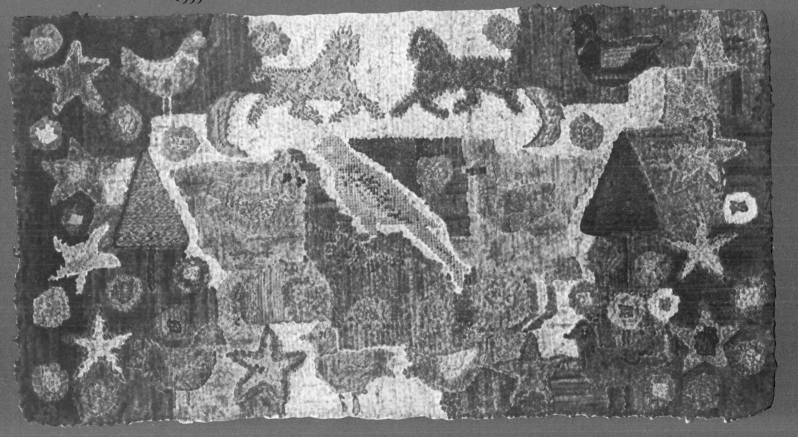

2000

1995 *A simple and honest composition in which horse and fencing tell the story* 1996 *Eagle and shield are loosely rendered, with stars and circles adding extra decoration, c. 1800* 1997 *Pair of roosters framed in a charming border of leaf-clad serpentine vines. Made in Pennsylvania* 1998 *The dog is rendered in a flat tone, with no attempt at anatomical details* 1999 *Many birds, hens, horses, stars, and flowers blend into an unusually pleasant composition* 2000 *Two elephants, a house, circles, and patches of bushes are combined with originality into a crazy-quilt arrangement, 1897*

539

Heirlooms from Old Looms

2002

THOSE WHO SPIN and weave by hand find themselves part of the continuity of history, as textile processes are among the oldest and most important inventions of ancient man. To this continuous record, the women of America have made a lasting contribution. From the earliest days to well into the nine-teenth century, Colonial women, starting with the shearings of sheep and the cuttings of flax, wove the coarse fibers into articles of beauty and utility.

Hand spinning is the process of converting fibers into a form of yarn, thread, or string. The best-known animal fibers in Colonial America came from sheep and rabbit fur. The

2001 *Eighteenth-century loom on which the home weaver made her homespun bedspreads, cover-lets, floor runners, and other materials was a crudely built affair, yet substantial enough to withstand the continual stresses of the weaving process. The professional weaver, working in his shop, used the same general type of loom. His, however, was equipped with more harnesses—from four to as many as twelve. Photograph courtesy Colonial Williamsburg* **2002** *Ever-popular rose motif in symmetrical design scheme, c. 1840* **2003, 2004** *Woven on Jacquard looms, these coverlets are typical; large central area carries borders on four sides of the bedspreads, c. 1835–40*

2003   2004

2005

2006

2007

2008

only vegetable fibers grown were flax and hemp. Yarn was a loosely spun fiber, while thread designated a fiber more tightly spun and twisted. More accurately, the product of man's earliest attempts to make thread may be described as string, which resulted from separating fibers with the fingers and twisting them into the strength or thickness needed. Without spinning there could be no weaving; without fibers there could be no spinning. Fortunately, early laws produced an abundance of the basics for spinning and weaving. In Massachusetts, for example, an ordinance of the 1640s made it compulsory for each Colonial family to spin a given quantity of yarn every year or face a penalty of heavy fines. Growing flax and raising sheep were urgent economic necessities. At home the making of cloth was both essential and inevitable. Sir Henry Moore, governor of New York in the 1760s, wrote: "Every house swarms with children who are set to work as soon as they are able to Spin and Card, and as every family is furnished with a Loom, Itinerant Weavers then put the finishing hand on the work."

In every Colonial home there was the sound of the whirling spinning wheel. To prepare wool for the high, or "walking," wheel on which it was spun into yarn, the heavy winter fleece of the sheep was processed through an arduous succession of cleaning, carding, and combing. The spinning was done on a large wheel; flax was spun on a smaller wheel, also known as a Saxon wheel, a tiring chore often performed by the man of the house. The desired flax fibers were separated by soaking, pounding, scraping, or combing. After the woolen yarn was spun, it was wound into hanks on a wooden frame called a niddy nod-dy, about two feet long.

The large loom on which the yarns or threads were woven into cloth was usually the work of the local carpenter. It occupied a space in the attic, a separate shed, or a special loom room. When space was at a premium the contrivance, sometimes built by the master of the house, was placed in the kitchen, where it occupied about the area of a four-poster bed. The mysteries of weaving—of warp and woof, of heddle and shuttle—were carried on for long hours in order to produce the simple fabrics needed to clothe the members of the family, or to provide the basic material for all bedding and coverlets.

The simplest loom consisted of a frame into which pegs or nails were driven at top or bottom. The warp threads, stretched vertically, were the strongest, and usually made of a better grade of thread than the crosswise threads, called the woof or weft. The warp threads were fastened on the loom like strings on a harp; the woof threads were then worked in and out or across with the fingers, a needle, or a shuttle. In a more advanced type of loom there was a mechanism which separated the warp threads. This action formed a shed, or V-shaped trough, through which the shuttle containing the weft thread was passed from side to side. The warp threads of the trough then recrossed each other to make a new shed. Each time the warp crossed, it locked and held the weft thread just placed in the trough. On some hand looms and on all mechanized looms, the shuttle carrying the weft thread was attached to a spring or propelled by one so that it was shot through, or seemed to fly through the shed instead of being pushed through. This was a fly-shuttle loom, on which it was possible to

2009

weave much faster.

The weaving of patterns, in contrast to simple unpatterned fabrics, called for more than two sets of heddles and harnesses and threads of different colors. The foot loom, introduced during the early seventeenth century, had various pedals with which to work the crossbars, thus leaving the hands free to manipulate the shuttle. The draw loom was invented to produce intricate patterns. Here the many sets of heddles were operated by cords pulled by a small boy, who had to swing about precariously, monkey-fashion, atop the large loom. In 1784 Edmund Cartwright invented the power loom, which performed all the operations of moving the heddles and shuttle in any manner desired. This English clergyman, with no knowledge of weaving and very little of mechanics, made a major contribution to lessening the burdens of the tedious hand operations.

The coloring of the fabrics and yarns used by Colonial women was often done by the overworked housewife, who used dyes concocted from various plants in her garden. Red came in various shades and hues as produced by the pokeberry, dogwood, sumac, cherry, and bloodroot; the latter was a favorite with the Indians, who used it to paint their faces and decorate their clothing. Orange came from bittersweet and sassafras bark, yellow from onionskins. Blue, always a popular color in Colonial needlework, usually came from the

indigo plant, either grown domestically in the South or imported. Green was derived from the pressed blossoms of the goldenrod; purple came from blueberries and iris petals. "Butternut brown," the term invariably used to describe the early settlers' garments, was obtained from the bark of the butternut tree. Thus, with the exception of indigo, practically all colors came from indigenous plants. indigo, a permanent dark blue, was a perennial favorite, especially for coverlets and linsey-woolsey. It was in such demand that special "indigo peddlers" earned their living selling it from door to door.

2010

In the early Colonial period, all cloth required by the average family was made by the housewife, with the help of the children. Later, a great deal of weaving was carried on by traveling journeymen. (The term derived from the fact that the "journey" represented a day's work; in other words, these craftsmen were paid a day's wages.) They relieved the housewife of her tedious weaving and also helped somewhat in pottery making, carpentry, tailoring, and various other crafts. They were an enlivening influence throughout the Colonies, and were depended upon to supply vivid gossip about neighbors an` other places. Finally, the weaving shop and the professional weaver became a part of each commu...ty, and women ordered fabrics from the weaver though they still furnished him with yarn.

2011

2012

2005–2012 *Details selected at random from woven coverlets show many favorite motifs: conventionalized tree and gateposts, basket of fruit and flowers, lion, eagle with motto, horses, tree, plowman from coverlet called Farmer's Fancy, and eagle with stars*

2013

The patterns for weaving, sometimes recorded on paper, were called "drafts," and were passed from family to family, generation to generation, and town to town. These patterns, like folk stories and legends, were modified gradually by the more creative persons until the originals were changed beyond recognition—a process of evolution common to all arts and crafts. Originally these drafts were brought to this country by immigrant weavers from Britain, Scotland, Germany, and Scandinavia, where weaving and needlecraft were particularly strong. Except to an expert weaver, the elaborate written instructions were meaningless. To the weaver they spelled out the rhythm and pattern one feels in musical compositions.

Handwoven coverlets, whether made at home by members of the family or by the professional or journeyman weaver, may be classified into several categories, according to type and technique involved. These are, in order of their complexity, the overshot, also known as float weave; the summer-and-winter weave; the block or double-weave geometric; and the so-called Jacquard weave.

2014

The overshot weave was one of the earliest and was of three-thread construction. There was one warp, usually a two-ply linen or cotton; a binder weft, in the same material as the warp but often a single ply and slightly smaller in grist; and the pattern weft, which was a colored woolen yarn. The pattern of the overshot was three-toned: dark, light, and a halftone. The dark spots or blocks forming the real design were composed of several wefts, where they overlay the basic linen or cotton ground. These are called floats, skips, or overshots. Most frequently this type of coverlet is in a four-block pattern. The overshot design has produced some of our finest and most interesting pure geometrics.

Coverlets woven in the summer-and-winter weave were so named because of their reversible two-toned pattern. They did not have as wide a distribution as the overshot weave and were to be found primarily in the Pennsylvania and New York areas, brought over originally, it is said, by the German immigrants of the early eighteenth century. Because of the intricacy of the patterns, the looms on which these coverlets were woven used eight or sixteen harnesses and called for expert weaving techniques. Indigo blue was favored, contrasting white or natural linen with the dark blue motifs; the design which appeared in blue on one side was reversed and appeared in white on the opposite side. The pattern was still geometric but more intricate than the overshot. The threads were bound together tightly, and it was structurally sounder than the overshot weave. This type of coverlet disappeared at an early date because of the extreme complexity of its execution.

The professional weaver, whether he was an itinerant journeyman or conducted his affairs in his own shop, was responsible for the type of coverlet called block or double-woven geometric, since an elaborate loom was required. These block coverlets, produced mainly from 1820 to 1840, were often the work of German or Scottish weavers, who had pattern books in their native lands featuring the designs; a few of these books were brought over to America. For coloration, they followed the popular style of that day, favoring indigo blue woolen yarn, usually supplied by the

2013–2015 *Pure geometric patterns result in an infinite number of variations as produced in the overshot technique of weaving. Dark wool lies on the light warp, skipping a number of threads; hence the name "overshot." Heavy weft* 2015 *threads and thin warp produce an uneven surface, so that there are textural as well as pattern variants*

2016

2017

housewife, combined with a factory-made, natural-colored cotton yarn which the weaver supplied. Red and blue yarns were sometimes used together, giving a patriotic aspect to the coverlet.

The fancy flowered coverlets, the Jacquard, include some of the most magnificent designs in the field of American weaving. These first appeared around 1820, particularly in New York and Pennsylvania, later spreading westward into Ohio, Kentucky, Indiana, and Illinois. It is the opinion of most students that the early examples were produced by professional weavers on the draw loom, while later ones were made on hand-operated looms with the aid of the Jacquard attachment. Featured in this general type of coverlet was a wide variety of floral motifs, employed both in diapered arrangements and freely chosen groupings of roses and tulips, laurel, and other leafy ornaments. The borders on the drop sides of these spreads were elaborate and striking, utilizing many finely rendered patriotic motifs. There were stars, shields, eagles, ribbons, mottoes, and figures of George Washington, as well as Mount Vernon and the

2018

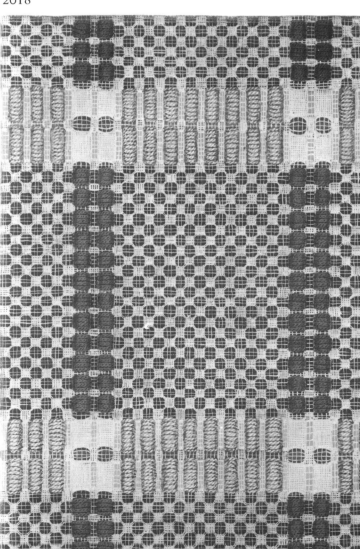

546

Capitol. Accompanying these were strong chauvinistic urgings: "United We Stand, Divided We Fall," "Under this eagle, we prosper," "Agriculture & Manufactures Are the Foundation of our Independence." It was customary for the weaver to place the date and his name, or that of the individual for whom the coverlet was made, in a corner of the border. In many cases, both names were included, as well as the town or county where the coverlet was woven. This invaluable imprimatur has eliminated all guesswork about the coverlet's provenance.

2016–2021 *Woolen coverlets woven by women from Maine to Georgia and west into Indiana and Illinois were given names as picturesque as the diversified regions in which they were made. Some small idea may be gained by listing just a few: Indian March, Braddock's Defeat, Cuckoo's Nest, Maid of Orleans, Bonaparte's Retreat, Broken Snowballs, and so on. Names were changed to suit the temperament and dialect of each region. A pattern called Sea Star or Seashell in one part of Tennessee became Isle of Patmos and Gentleman's Fancy in another. When such liberties are taken and such differences occur, it is impossible to identify any overshot pattern by a specific name*

2019

2020

2021

547

2022

2022–2029 *Coverlets made from Jacquard weaves are usually reversible, one side light and the other dark. The weaver's name was often woven into one corner, with his address and the date. If the coverlet was made to order, the*

2026

548

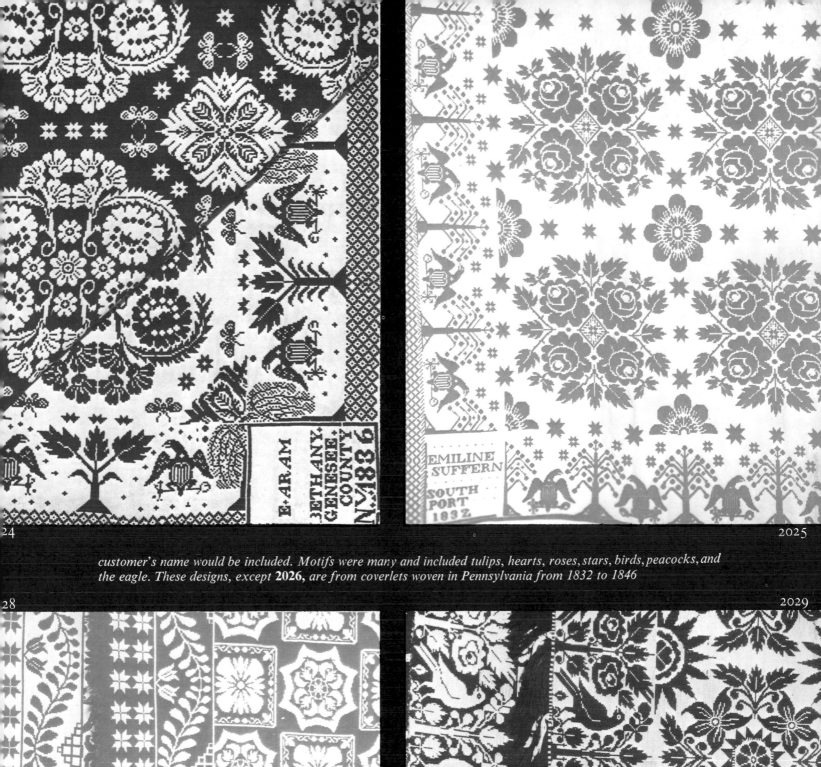

*customer's name would be included. Motifs were many and included tulips, hearts, roses, stars, birds, peacocks, and the eagle. These designs, except **2026**, are from coverlets woven in Pennsylvania from 1832 to 1846*

549

2030

2031

2030–2037 *Patriotic motifs appear on many coverlets; the eagle is always present, sometimes accompanied by stars, a figure of Washington, or slogans and mottoes,* **2033, 2035, 2036.** *The well-known Boston Town pattern appears in* **2030,** *with yet another adaptation of this in* **2034.** *Florals, paired peacocks, and rose clusters are shown in* **2031, 2034,** *and* **2037,** *dated 1840 to 1858*

2034

2035

2032

2033

2036

2037

2038

2038 The Quilting Party, *painted by an unknown artist, c. 1840–50. It pictures an important social event; the final sewing into place of the many blocks and friendship pieces of the quilt. It was an occasion for festive animation, a time for the gathering of young and old in meetinghouse or schoolroom. Courtesy the Abby Aldrich Rockefeller Folk Art Collection, Williamsburg, Virginia* **2039** *The spinning wheel was a fixture in every Colonial home. After the winter fleece was sheared from the sheep's back, it was processed through many stages of cleaning, carding, and combing. Then the loose fibers were deftly twisted at the wheel into continuous strands for weaving* **2040** *Quilts were made up of units like this, sewn together for a large bedspread. This is a mosaic calico piece, made in 1810 near Corning, New York*

The Quilting Bee

2039

2040

No WOMAN EVER quilted alone if she could help it. The quilting bee provided an opportunity for women to gather and gossip. When the bee was held in a grange hall or church vestry room, as many as twelve women could attend. Usually, however, the number of guests was limited to seven, who, with the hostess, made up two quilting frames, the equivalent of two tables of bridge. Good quilting in earlier times was a social requisite, and it behooved the ambitious woman to be an expert with her needle.

The quilting frame was a simple homemade affair, much like today's curtain stretcher. The frame held the patchwork securely so that the decorative top quilt, the inner lining of cotton or wool, and the backing could be sewn together. The quilt was "rolled" from each of the four sides until the center was reached and the quilt completed. Often several quilts were finished in a single session which lasted all day. These sessions ended with a supper of roast chicken or turkey. The men usually arrived in time for the feast, after which there followed singing and dancing. Like so many well-

2041

2042

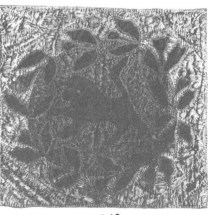

2043

established rural customs—apple-paring bees, corn-husking contests, and barn-raising parties —the traditional quilting party carried with it all of the social amenities. The event marked the successful completion of many months of laborious handiwork.

Several forms of coverlet were derived from European backgrounds; they followed traditional patterns and displayed regional variations. The patchwork quilt, however, made from cotton, calico, and silk fragments, was a distinctly American invention—an economic necessity. The need to salvage every scrap of material and to piece these scraps together to form attractive patterns of beauty and ingenuity constituted an original folk art. Whereas affluent women could import bolts of English materials or patronize specialty shops, those with limited resources had to improvise, making patterns from their carefully hoarded remnants. These are the prized heirlooms in today's needlecraft collections.

There were many techniques of quilting. Pieced or patchwork quilts, first made in the latter part of the eighteenth century, are those in which the patterns follow geometrical designs—mosaics laboriously contrived of hundreds of small squares and diamonds. At first these small pieces were sewn directly onto a fabric backing, but by 1800 women had developed a more practical method and made the quilt parts in block units, each a portion of the overall design scheme. These blocks were pieced together in rows or diagonal bands, with strips of latticework or alternate white blocks between them. When plain white blocks were used as alternate separations, they were also elaborately quilted.

The patterns for quilting were indicated on the material by pencil, chalk, or charcoal, depending on the color of the fabric. Since it was easier to seam two straight edges, the geometric pattern evolved along straight lines running laterally or diagonally or emanating radially from a central point. Thousands of designs resulted and each had its own fanciful name. Often a single pattern was given different names in widely separated regions, nor was it uncommon to find the same name applied to several unrelated designs. For example, Bear's Paw in Ohio, or Duck Feet in

2041–2046 *Quilt blocks were a practical solution in the making of a large spread; the small panels were easily manageable and could be assembled at the quilting bee, if necessary. It was the custom for makers of separate "friendship blocks" to sign their names to the pieces, an added sentimental remembrance for the quilt owner. Dated 1870*

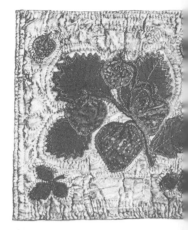

2044

2045

2046

2041

2042

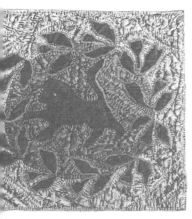

2043

the Mud on Long Island, became Hand of Friendship in Pennsylvania. There are star patterns named for every state in the Union derived from the basic Star of Bethlehem, an eight-pointed star found in numerous interpretations. Entire volumes have been devoted to describing these quilts with quaint and charming names, which included such whimsies as Hen and Chickens, Flying Geese, Stepping Stones, Birds in the Window, Delectable Mountains, Rose of Sharon, Flying Dutchman, Cats and Mice, Turkey Tracks, Jacob's Ladder, Drunkard's Path, Road to California, Robbing Peter to Pay Paul, Young Man's Fancy, Philadelphia Pavement, Jack-in-the-Pulpit, Chimney Swallows, Hearts and Gizzards, and Rolling Stone.

The patchwork counterpanes of the nineteenth century were usually made of solid-colored or printed cotton fabrics, alternating with white for contrast. A favorite color scheme combined turkey red with green cotton, appliquéd on white. Quilted stitching on the white background—perhaps in a lozenge diaper pattern or in squared criss-crossing—provided textural interest to the plain areas. No matter how elaborate the patchwork designs, the stitching of the quilted portions greatly enhanced the attractiveness of the spread. This was the gauge by which quilts were judged in contests. Quilting rather than piecing required the highest degree of needlework. Some women were superior in cutting and sewing the patches, but could never quite master the quilting techniques, which required true ambidexterity. The ultimate in skillful needlework often appears on the all-white counterpanes, where, in the absence of color and bright designs, only the delicate finesse of expert needlecraft is evident.

Toward the middle of the nineteenth century, the social aspects of quilting and the popularity of quilting parties resulted in group

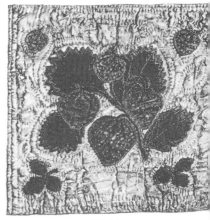

2044

2045

2046

2047

2047, 2048 *The Star of Bethlehem, an intriguing pattern involving difficult piecing and endless patience, has had great attraction for oldtime quilt makers. The making of the star called for thousands of diamond-shaped pieces of chintz, calico, and copperplate fabrics, carefully chosen for color blending and harmony. The eight-pointed star had four corners and four triangles to be designed and pieced according to personal whims, but the dominant motif of the Star held real fascination*

2048

needlecraft for the making of signature, friendship, autograph, bride, album, and presentation quilts. Each quilt was generally intended for a special person or special occasion and conveyed the sentiments of the well-wishers. The donor or originator of the quilt planned the basic outline and assigned separate blocks to friends in the group. When the blocks were completed, the group gathered for a sociable afternoon to assemble the quilt, with its embroidered signatures or good wishes. The honored guest might have been a minister or his wife, an esteemed citizen, or a bride. The variety of designs and expressions of a dozen or more women produced a most interesting memento. The interrelationship of the separate pieces created an ensemble of rare loveliness, quite revealing as an exercise in original folk arts and crafts.

The technique of producing appliqué quilt-

2049

2050

2049 *Quilt involving twenty-five squares proved a challenging invitation for the quilt maker to express her decorative talents* **2050** *Sixteen component floral units, bordered by a swag motif with tulips, show a genuine sense of design and originality* **2051** *Appliqué motifs consist of red flowers and green leaves on white muslin. The central motif of hearts forms a star, in turn encircled by two whirling wheels of leaf and floral forms, typically Pennsylvania German, 1848* **2052** *Friendship quilt in which the outer squares are cut into halves as an interesting variant* **2053** *Floral wreaths and plants decorate this quilt, including a lemon and an orange tree flanking the central diamond, which is a pictorial motif of the owner's house and garden* **2054** *Baskets of flowers and posies of gay-colored chintzes are further embellished by gracefully twisting vines* **2055** *Appliquéd units of calico and chintz are composed of large, flat masses simply outlined* **2056** *Mexican Rose pattern is executed in brilliant red, yellow, and green on white field of shells and feathers*

ing differed somewhat from that of patchwork, though often the two methods were combined in a single spread. Strictly speaking, patchwork produced a mosaic textile; appliqué was constructed from individual pieces which were sewn to a background fabric. The central part of the design sometimes contained a large single unit like the Tree of Life. More often, a smaller unit was repeated in diaper fashion four, nine, or sixteen times to cover the quilt area. Chintz or other printed cotton was cut up to form the decorative elements and added lively interest to the plain fabrics. The Rose of Sharon was a design favorite as it was a

2051

2052

2053

2054

bride's quilt, the final piece in her hope chest. The beauty of this design echoed the tender good wishes of those who made the quilt and presented it to the bride.

By 1850 appliquéd patchwork had become so elaborate that it was too precious for everyday use. The quilts became counterpanes or showpieces, ceasing to serve as coverlets. The pristine condition of many outstanding examples testifies to their limited use and these owe their survival to that custom.

A study of the more intricate appliquéd quilts will show why years often went into their making. Smaller units like the Orange Peel, Caesar's Crown, Basket of Tulips, Little Red Schoolhouse, or, for that matter, any unit repeated forty or fifty times for the quilt's central area involved the most work. The completion of such a quilt could easily have taken hundreds of hours. During the Civil War and the period that followed, there was a decline in quilt making. The introduction of machinery in the textile industry eliminated the need for such tedious needlework. The friendship quilt and its sentiments, along with woven coverlets and appliquéd masterpieces, became treasured heirlooms, testaments to a folk art that has all but vanished.

2055

2056

2057

2057 *Floral wreath, horn of plenty, and basket of flowers are further embellished with the introduction of the flag and eagle, pineapple, Bible, doves, and lyre—a complete grammar of decoration
expressing the sentimental lore of midnineteenth-century life* 2058–2063 *Squares of calico show
the simple elements of which large spreads were composed* 2064 *Floral wreaths, always, popular,
enabled the quilt maker to express her love of color and imagination in a garden fantasy* 2065
Basket of flowers, a perennial favorite in patterns, arranged with geometric simplicity

2058

2059

2060

2061

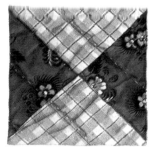

2062

2063

2064

2065

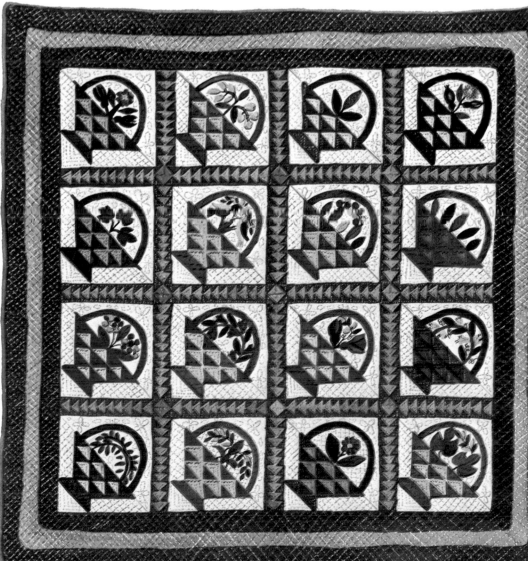

2066

2067

2066 *Basket of flowers, in appliqué, is outlined in quilting on white muslin background, 1820* **2067** *Appliquéd motifs in flat, solid pieces—reds, greens, and browns* **2068** *Morning-glory design in padded appliqué, with festooned border; quilted eagle on white, c. 1857* **2069** *Symmetrical flower-and-stem pattern in an all-over arrangement, within festooned*

2068

2069

2070

border **2070** *Padded quilting creates low relief in monochrome* **2071** *Sawtooth pattern called Delectable Mountains, with border of eagles, 1810* **2072** *Patchwork quilt of sunburst design, within border of swags and how knots, c. 1840. From photographs except 2066, 2071, and 2072*

2071   2072

2073

2074

2075

2076

2077

2078

2079

2073–2079 *Many accessories were needed to speed the work of spinning, weaving, and sewing. The spinning wheel,* **2703,** *is an essential prototype, varying only slightly in different models. The spinning reel,* **2075,** *was used for winding yarn into hanks. Among the quaint and decorative sewing objects,* **2076,** *the sewing bird of cast brass was used as a clamp for the edge of a table. The pads were for pincushions, while the springed beak could hold a piece of cloth till needed. The sewing machines shown,* **2077** *(1860),* **2078** *(1867), and* **2079** *(1858), are but a few of the dozens of new ones patented between the years 1850 and 1870. They were all of cast-iron construction, often gilded and decorated as if to apologize for the intrusion of a piece of mechanism into the Victorian household. The appliquéd piece, called "Gossips,"* **2074,** *introduces a humorous commentary in needlecraft by Eunice W. Cook, of Vermont*

2080

2081

2082

2083

2084

2085

2086

2080–2089 *Sewing tables, or work tables, as they were called, were made in a great number of styles. The delicately reeded model in the Sheraton style, **2080**, has a small top drawer and large compartment below; its top lifts at the front. The walnut sewing table, **2081**, with cabriole legs, is dated 1750–79. On the skirted models, a sliding shelf pulls out to expose the bag, **2085**, while the top sides lift up, **2086**. Sewing stands and spool racks are shown in **2082–84**. Sewing birds of wood and brass are to be seen in **2087–89***

2087

2088

2089

Teach Me To Love Another We
To Slide The Fox I See
Sr Mercy Too Others Show
That Mercy Shows To Me

Priscilla Nelsons Sampler Wrought In The
14 Year Of Her Age January 23 1837

A B C D E F G H I K
L M N O P Q R S
U V W X Y Z

Sentimental Samplers

2091

THERE IS a fascinating naiveté about folksy samplers. Students of early needlework have found a world of whimsy and frivolity in the untutored expressions of young girls exhibiting their sewing skills, displaying their knowledge of the Bible, or sharing their homespun philosophy. These pieces of handiwork became a part of a girl's dowry, traveled with her throughout life, and were willed to a favorite relative.

Before a young girl attended school to learn the three Rs, she was expected to be proficient in plain sewing, embroidery, and cross-stitching. She helped her mother with hems and seams, and filled in with minor needlecraft chores. At school she had rigid lessons in all techniques of needlework. By the time she was eight she was ready to start displaying her mastery of difficult stitches, her printing and handwriting, her sense of rhythm and composition on a canvas. The sampler was a rou-

2090 *The sampler provided a young girl with a great opportunity for self-expression. This exercise demonstrates her ability to handle the alphabet, adding a bit of doggerel and a pictorial scene—all enclosed in a decorative floral border, made in 1837* **2091** *Stitching embroidery on coarse buckram or canvas imparted some geometrical limitations that added charm and style to the sampler*

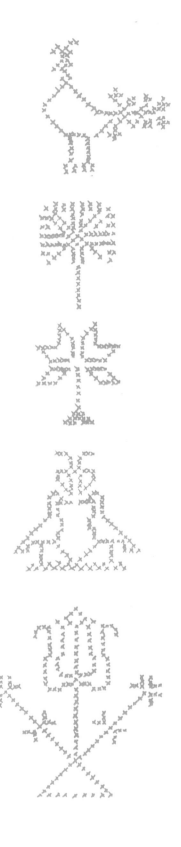

tine part of every Pilgrim daughter's upbringing, proof of her spelling ability and her parents' spiritual influence.

One of the earliest extant samplers, dated 1653, was the work of Lora Standish, daughter of Captain Miles Standish. Very few seventeenth-century samplers survive today, but we have much evidence of diligent handicraft from the 1750s until about 1840. The first samplers were on long strips of handwoven linen about eight inches wide, and the alphabet was almost invariably the dominating element. Fruits and flower sprays were used as borders or to fill in a short line. Horizontal bands made full use of vines and serpentine scrolls interspersed with stylized units. Birds, animals, figures, and architectural facades served as main themes, sometimes dominating the lettering. As time passed, the emphasis changed and alphabetical arrangements were supplanted by essentially pictorial formats, especially in the more ambitious efforts of older children and adults. Beginners had to stick to their ABCs until they acquired proficiency in both composition and needlecraft. Favorite motifs included the Tree of Life, fleur-de-lis, trefoil, Indian pink, pineapple, strawberry, acorn, and various common tree forms.

Typical eighteenth-century samplers, most of which were made in New England, show several different styles of the alphabet, sometimes as many as five. Roman letters were common. A more florid or cursive set of capital letters sometimes preceded those; then, for greater variety, an alphabet of script letters followed. Numerals were sometimes shown if a line needed filling. The most important test of mastery of letter forms came with the handling of a motto or inscription, the fillip that gave expression to the creative spirit and added a literary touch.

Quotations from the Scriptures, the Lord's Prayer, the Apostles' Creed, and the Ten Commandments were used frequently. Other verses dealt with themes of love and friendship, maidenhood and chastity, death and

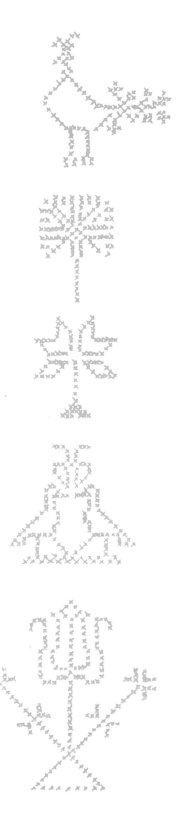

sorrow. Late nineteenth-century samplers follow the prevailing sentiments of the Victorian era, elevating the sanctity of the home, the sweetness of friendship, familial unity, and heavenly protection. Mottoes could be sternly moralistic or graciously benevolent: "Give us this day our daily bread"; "Thou, O God, seest all"; and "Remember the Sabbath day to keep it Holy." Simple and effective as these mottoes were, they did not adequately afford full expression of sentiment. The young Victorian lass preferred verse, which seemed to her more expressive. There were many source books that served as exemplars of sampler verse: *Godey's, Harper's Magazine,* the many editions of the *Ladies' Album,* and Isaac Watts' *Divine Songs for Children.*

The central theme of the sampler took on greater importance toward the middle of the eighteenth century. As early as 1709 the Adam and Eve motif, a perennial favorite, appeared; another example is dated 1741. In both of these the main figures are nude. In another treatment of the celebrated couple, in 1760, they appear in Quaker costume; the scene also includes a Brown University building and a doctor's gig and horse. Other samplers show further variants of this motif, with fig tree, flowers, and animals. Many Biblical scenes were stitched, among them Noah's Ark and the Holy Land. The hunting scene was one more popular pictorial device that could show to advantage a variety of animals, birds, dogs in pursuit, and stags at bay. An unusual sampler suggesting a family record features a charming pattern of decorative squares in which sprays of flowers alternate with pious sentiments.

About the middle of the eighteenth century, a house or church became the central feature around which a composition was planned. Gardens, trees, and picket fences offered opportunities for interesting color treatment. An architectural motif in the hands of a young and unsophisticated artist could become a joy in

Jesus permit thy gracious name to stand
As the first effort of a youthful hand,
And while her fingers oer the canvas move
Engage her tender heart to seek thy love.

Mary. S.C. Burchfield. East Liberty.

2092

2093

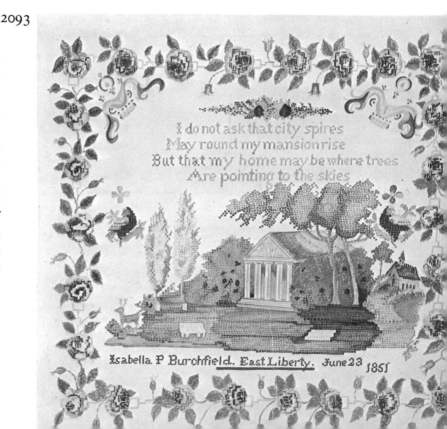

I do not ask that city spires
May round my mansion rise
But that my home may be where trees
Are pointing to the skies

Isabella P Burchfield. East Liberty. June 23 1851

its simple rendition, reflecting the contemporary scene with sincerity. Buildings appear frequently beginning about 1745 and continuing for about a hundred years. There was a tendency to illustrate mansions rather than humble cottages. Whether this indicated that the makers were residents or whether it merely represented their hopes and aspirations is a matter of conjecture. One of the most masterful treatments was achieved by Anna Pierce of Oxford, Massachusetts. Her sampler features the typical dwelling of her day, complete with elliptical fanlight over the handsome doorway

2094

2092 *The most popular form of sampler combined the alphabet, some pictorial representation, a decorative border of nature motifs, and the maker's signature* 2093 *Sampler in crewel stitching with woolen threads on linen, dated 1851* 2094 *Sampler on canvas base embroidered in silk floss and twist, c. 1795* 2095 *Sampler of linen needlework, c. 1799* 2096 *Sampler embroidered on linen scrim, c. 1821*

2095

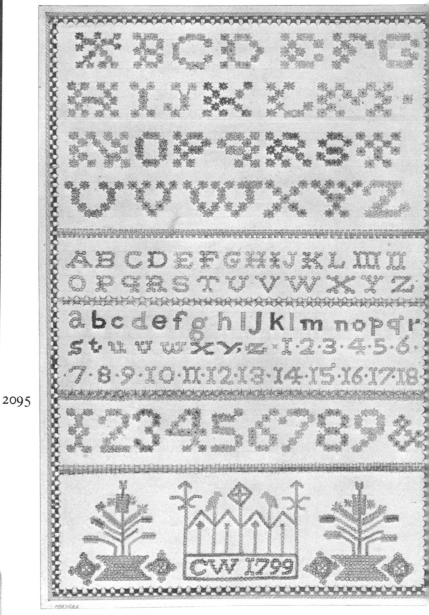

2096

and a white picket fence. Many a young artist had difficulty with perspective and drew the sides of the house with total disregard for its principles, but therein lies some of the charm. Schoolhouses and public buildings also proved of interest. New York's City Hall, topped by a six-line verse, is the subject of a large pictorial sampler. Although the architectural details were highly stylized and fenestration greatly simplified, the representation is faithful and unmistakable.

573

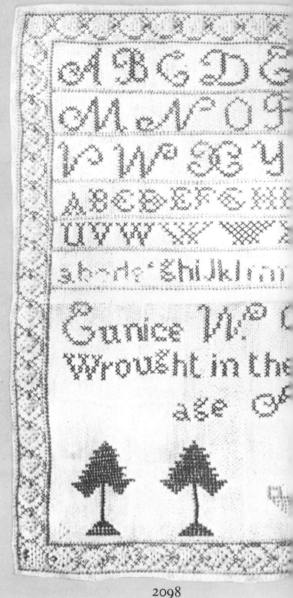

2098

2097

2099

2100

574

2101

2097–2102 Sampler designs varied as much as the personalities that made them. Some samplers were composed merely to display skill in handling the alphabet in Roman or script letters, both capitals and minuscules, 2098 and 2100. Others show preference for ornamentation or pictures, 2099, 2101, 2102; the last is almost tapestry-like in effect

2102

575

2103

2103 *Printed textiles on a political theme were a way of popularizing a president or a nominee. In this all-over pattern printed on cotton, c. 1830, the first seven presidents of the United States appear, with dates of their administrations. This was based upon an earlier French toile inscribed "Les Présidents des États-Unis," but the original does not show the portrait of Jackson nor does it have the spread eagle at the left or the frigate* Constitution *on the right. These adaptations exemplify the copying of historical subject matter from engravings* **2104** *Literally hundreds of commemorative designs were printed on cotton, linen, or silk depicting portraits of George Washington or scenes from his life*

2104

Commemorative Cotton & Chintz

THE ICONOGRAPHY of American history on cloth probably started within a year of the Revolution, in 1777, possibly with a cotton kerchief attributed to John Hewson of Philadelphia depicting George Washington as commander in chief of the Continental army. As with most textile prints of the period, it was not an entirely original creation; it was based upon a published engraving by C. Shepherd dated September 9, 1775.

There was an active coterie of at least twenty copperplate engravers producing paper prints in the Colonies before the Revolution. Immediately following the war their numbers increased rapidly, as the demand for historical engravings in the young republic continued to grow. The later engravers concerned themselves with recording the heroes and battles of the Revolution, and thereafter the War of 1812. Plate after plate glorified the exploits of the infant navy. When Jackson managed to win the only major land victory, at New Orleans, that triumph was celebrated with prints by four different engravers.

The ease with which engravers could turn out prints on single sheets of dampened paper could not be achieved in printing bolts of cloth; for this it was necessary to engrave the designs on calenders or rolls.

Reflecting the vogue abroad, printed cottons of all types were in use in America as early as the middle of the seventeenth century, but they were imported from England, which strictly prohibited the manufacture and printing of cottons in the Colonies. By the early part of the eighteenth century, however, many Colonists fretting at the restrictive policy openly violated the ban. Benjamin Franklin's elder brother James, in 1720, advertised in the *Boston Gazette:* "Linnens, Calicoes, Silks, etc. printed in good figures, very lively, and durable colors, and without the offensive smell which commonly attends the linens printed here." Not only were there frequent press notices showing that competition was keen in this trade, but textile printing tools were advertised. Francis Dewing, a Boston engraver, had let it be known in 1713 that he "Engraveth and Printeth copper Plates, likewise cuts neatly and printeth Calicoes."

Most ships arriving from England carried a substantial cargo of dry goods, which were bought up as soon as they were unloaded. Colonial visitors to Britain rarely failed to purchase prints for room furnishings, curtains, bed hangings, or materials for a lady's costume. Another early reference to copperplate prints comes from Benjamin Franklin in a letter to his wife from London in 1758: "There are also fifty-six yards of cotton, printed curiously from copper plates, a new invention, to make bed and window curtains; and seven yards of chair bottoms, printed in the same way, very neat. This was my fancy, but Mrs. Stevenson tells me I did wrong not to buy both of the same color."

The early designs from abroad had followed the traditional floral patterns and other themes of nature. When the Revolution stimulated a market for commemorative subject matter, the printers of cotton goods at first concerned themselves with portraits and with episodes in the life of Washington, the Revolution, and the Federal period. Then followed the War of 1812, genre subjects on the American theme, transportation and the conquest of the West, and political campaigns of the forties and fifties. Pictorial maps, the Civil War, and finally, late in the century, expositions supplied material for broadsides, kerchiefs, and yard goods. But the popularity of such subjects waned as each event slowly passed into history. The designers of cotton goods often took their cue from current best-selling Currier and Ives lithographs; in repetition there was safety.

The limited parallel between graphics and print goods ends with the matter of subject interest. As color and fashion trends changed, the mills of New England, in order to keep abreast of competition, found it expedient to gauge their markets carefully to insure survival, and it was the role of the industrial designer to make his contribution to this end.

2105 *Historical print on buff-colored linen called* The Apotheosis of Franklin, *made c. 1780–83*

2106

2107

2106–2111 Cottons, especially chintzes and calicoes, in an endless variety of patterns and color schemes were being produced in great yardage by the third decade of the nineteenth century. The process of textile printing had made giant strides and centered around a few mill towns in Massachusetts, particularly Merrimac, whose works employed hundreds of hands. Expert craftsmen imported from England included designers, engravers, printers, color mixers, and chemists. Historical designs continued in great demand, changing in content with new presidents, campaigns, and slogans, and with the coming of the Civil War. In addition to the topical themes, such colorful subject as florals, agricultural scenes and settings, and homely episodes based upon everyday life were popular

2108

2109

2110

2111

2112

2113

2114

2115

2116

2117

2118

2119

2120

2121

2122

2112–2122 *The constantly recurring use of George Washington as a theme, 2112, 2113, 2117, and 2122, is a testament to his immortality as a design symbol. William Penn's treaty with the Indians is featured in 2120. William Harrison, the military hero, is shown in 2116, while his log cabin at North Bend, Ohio, is depicted in 2115, on a cotton printed in 1841. Scenes from the Mexican War and Zachary Taylor at the Battle of Palo Alto are shown in 2114 and 2121. Transportation in a country gaining an awareness of its magnitude is featured in the scene of the canal boat with passengers and the Mississippi river scene, which pictures a stern-wheeler with cotton fields in the foreground, c. 1825–30*

2123

2124

2125

2126

2123–2128 *Floral prints and fabrics used for a variety of household drapery and chair coverings, bedspreads, and children's dress goods display in infinite variety the garden favorites of roses, carnations, peonies, tulips, daisies, morning glories, and many others. Realism is favored except in the whimsies pictured in 2123 and the stylized version of a coverlet in 2124. The eagle spreads his wings in 2127 and 2128*

2128

2127

2129

2130

2131

2132

2133

2134

2135

2136

2137

GALLERY OF TEXTILES. *All-over patterns, 2130–2140, achieve a continuous harmony by repetition of the same unit. The pleasant ornamental effect depends upon a rhythmic flow of decorative elements, blending and weaving into one another. Foliage, vines, and arboreal motifs, interspersed with floral sprigs and leafy sprays, with the introduction of birds or animals for added realistic excitement, were perennial favorites for home use. In 2137 and 2138, a badminton court and winter-sports scenes illustrate the occasional use of genre subjects*

2138

2140

2139

BOOK
FIVE

Children's World

BOOK FIVE: *Children's World*

2141

2141 The Circus *was painted in 1874. by A. Logan, National Gallery of Art, Washington, D.C. Gift of Edgar William and Bernice Chrysler Garbisch.* **2142** *The circus wagon* The Golden Age of Chivalry, *designed by George Lawrence of the Sebastian Wagon Company, was built c. 1887–89*

The Circus Comes to Town

2142

HURRY! HURRY! HURRY!" has been the raucous cry of the big-top barker ever since John Robinson hauled the first traveling show, consisting of three wagons, five horses, and a tent, beyond the Alleghenies in 1824. Before the nineteenth century ended, the American circus had become not only "The Greatest Show on Earth" but a big business which involved dozens of touring troupes, thousands of performers, and animals from all parts of the globe. This was the heyday of the circus, roughly from 1875 to 1915, with its dazzling three rings, its freaks, and its spangles, glitter, and noise.

The magnificent prologue to the main show was the mile-long parade in a slow, well-ordered procession from the railroad yards to the big tent. The brightly decorated circus wagons carried clowns, musicians, lady per-

formers, and animal cages. The steam calliopes sounded a brassy cacophony, and the clumsy, ten-ton *Two Hemispheres* wagon was drawn by a team of forty horses, while dozens of elephants, from midget to jumbo, marched linked together tail in trunk. Phineas T. Barnum inaugurated this parade of colorful circus wagons with the attendant ballyhoo. Favorite parade themes included allegories, legendary heroes of the golden age of chivalry, and Orientalia.

The few remaining circus wagons found today in museums and circus collections are reminders of those spectacles. These ponderous show pieces were created for glamour and showmanship; the over-ornamentation and excessive use of gilded scrolls were designed to captivate the eye. Yet beneath the tinsel and gilt were finely carved figures, symbols of the circus during its apogee. While the whole town usually turned out to see the "super-colossal, transcendentally amazing and electrifying feats of the most stupendous exhibition ever exploited," the gaudy show wagons bore silent testimony to the skills of woodcarvers and gilders.

Wood-carving served a special function in the circus world. The wood-carver, working on contract, turned out wagons with little of the glamour associated with a wood sculptor. The carvings on the wagons were not intended to be studied closely, but were designed primarily as a part of the passing spectacle. They reflected the influences that produced the eclectic and Baroque decorations of that day. Most circus carving was the work of untrained artists; it was not folk art but "popular art." The lavishly ornamented, highly colored wagons stimulated the visual senses and were the keynote of a transient style.

Barnum, Bailey, Cole, Forepaugh, and other circus owners were continually in need of new equipage because their wagons were exposed to all kinds of weather. The cost of the huge wagons could amount to thousands of dollars. Few firms, therefore, could be entrusted with these commissions. Samuel Robb of Canal Street, New York, and the Sebastian Wagon Company, also of New York, built the majority of the wagons. Other builders were located in Chicago, Leavenworth, Kansas, Germantown, Pennsylvania, and Tonawanda, New York.

Robb, sometimes working alone, built wagons and also carved figureheads and cigar-store figures. Later he worked for Sebastian, carving most of the important circus figures. He is known to have carved a series of nursery-rhyme and fairy-tale characters—Bluebeard, Cinderella, Mother Goose, Sindbad the Sailor, Red Riding Hood, and the Old Woman Who Lived in the Shoe—for the Barnum circus parade. Robb employed a few hands, among them Thomas White, who copied Classical statuary, producing a Greek slave and an Adam and Eve.

Many of the finest wagons were designed and built by Jacob Sebastian, a skilled carriagemaker who came to America from France in 1854. At the time of his death in 1880, his shop had grown to include a staff of carvers, figure painters, gilders, and letterers, in addition to carpenters, wainwrights, and wheelwrights. Until the decline of circus fortunes resulted in bankruptcy, Sebastian's son John continued the business, maintaining the staff and some vestige of his father's reputation.

In the construction of the wagons, oak and hickory were used for the structural members and frames and yellow pine and whitewood for most of the carvings. The softer woods were more vulnerable to exposure; this played great havoc with the carved figures, resulting in splitting, cracking, and the loss of arms, fingers, and noses. It is surprising, therefore, that any of these figures have survived. Van Amburgh's *Great Golden Chariot* was among the most lavish wagons. It was a richly carved structure which featured a helmeted, steel-armored noble slaying a lion with his lance,

2143 The Circus Coming into Town, *wood engraving by the illustrator team of Paul Frenzeny and Jules Tavernier, appeared in* Harper's Weekly, *October, 1873*

2144

surrounded by Romanesque scrolls. The Colmar brothers' prize wagon had a lifesize nude on each corner; these gilded showgirls never failed to create a stir in the audience. The Wallace Circus had a steam calliope with a high driver's seat flanked by ornate scrolls from which emerged a female figure driving stylized lions. Adam Forepaugh's steam calliope featured four over-lifesize figures of dancers and musicians holding tambourines and clarinets. The sides were ornamented with stylized eagles and snakes, or dragons. Barnum and Bailey's hand-carved calliope topped them all. The pipes emitted both steam and music and showed clearly through the latticed side panels, which had elliptical center medallions surmounted by carved cherubs riding on the spread-winged birds.

2145

2146

2144 *The circus wagon* United States *is one of the most magnificent examples of circus carving, replete with symbols of the American spirit. Figures and allegories proudly display the flag and the eagle. In the central panel the Goddess of Liberty stands flanked by Indian maidens. Every square foot is covered with architectural framework, arches and pilasters, arabesques and storied details designed to instill patriotic fervor in the hearts of spectators, c. 1875* **2145** *Seated lion carved in relief for a Sparks circus wagon, c. 1900* **2146** *Relief carving of figure with pipes of Pan, from circus wagon, c. 1900*

2147   2148

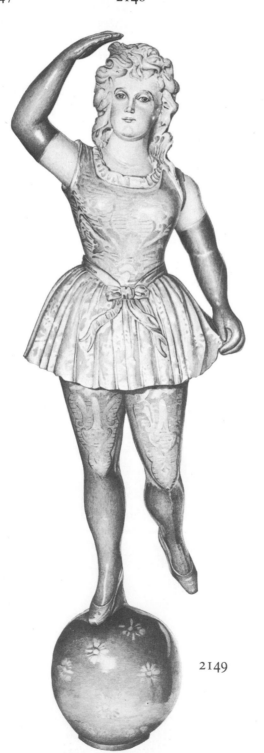

After the Barnum and Bailey show completed a successful five-year tour of Europe, Bailey decided to commemorate its triumph with the biggest and most elaborate gilded wagon in circus history, *Two Hemispheres*. The contract was awarded to Sebastian; its construction took almost a full year. One side of the wagon represented the eastern hemisphere and carried the emblems of Great Britain, France, Belgium, Spain, Italy, and Russia. On the other side, the United States, Canada, Mexico, Brazil, Argentina, and Chile were shown. A replica of the two hemispheres, guarded by a lion and a bear, was in the central portion. On the front, two American eagles appeared with outstretched wings, and on the rear were two elephant heads with uplifted trunks.

In a giant circus parade, at least a dozen wagons were drawn by matched teams of stallions in gay plumage and merrily tinkling bells. The bulk and weight of these circus wagons, so difficult to store and costly to maintain, have led to their destruction. Fortunately, a number of the wagons were stored on an empty farm lot outside of Bridgeport, Connecticut, some years ago. When storage charges

2149

2150

2151

began to mount and the circus company could not meet the payments, the wagons were put up for sale. At that time William Warren, state director of the WPA Federal Art Project, acquired the lot and its contents, thus salvaging many fine circus figures, which have since been acquired by collectors.

In addition to the few existing show wagons, numerous posters exist—from small handbills or throwaways with black-and-white engraved illustrations to gigantic four-sheet posters—which convey some of the grandeur and opulence of the circus in its heyday. The circus poster, never admired for its high level of artistry, was the only contemporary medium that adequately portrayed the details of the parades and the events of the circus.

2147–2150 *Circus wagons were designed to sparkle and glisten in the parade of floats and vehicles. Carving was in high relief; wagon sides were usually divided into architectonic units separated by pilasters, arches, and draped decorations. A special theme was assigned to a wagon:* **2147** *and* **2148** *show the Dolphin wagon. The Sparks wagon,* **2150,** *features a lyre and a winged head, with jesters behind and draperies at the sides. From photographs* **2149, 2152** *Calliope figures carved in the round, c. 1895* **2151** *Head carved by Sebastian Wagon Company for one of Barnum's circus wagons, c. 1885*

2152

599

2153   2154

2155   2156

2153, 2154 *Pair of dancing figures from Spark's circus wagon. Probably made by Moeller Brothers Wagon Company, Baraboo, Wisconsin, c. 1900* **2155, 2156** *Pair of draped figures, one with a lyre, the other holding a flower. They adorned the sides of Barnum and Bailey circus wagons made by the Sebastian Wagon Company of New York. Possibly carved by Samuel Robb, about 1880*

2157

2158

2159   2160

2157, 2158 *Pair of figures draped as muses, corner decorations on Barnum and Bailey circus wagon, c. 1880* **2159, 2160** *Figures carved by Samuel Robb of New York, noted for his cigar-store Indians of the same period, c. 1880*

2161

2162

Merry-Go-Round Menagerie

2163

THE FIRST REVOLVING platform with the carrousel figures we know today was built in the little town of North Tonawanda, New York, in 1879. The improvements, which included elaborate ornamentation and fanciful animals, heralded a new era. Previously, merry-go-rounds had featured only prancing horses and chariot seats. Carrousels, an entertainment feature of every fair here and abroad, were also an essential part of the circus, and they became the major attraction in amusement parks throughout the country, their numbers expanding rapidly during the closing years of the nineteenth century. Almost a dozen companies were kept busy turning out a veritable menagerie of wooden figures.

2161, 2162 Carrousel figures of a rooster and a lion. Photographs courtesy the Smithsonian Institution, Washington, D.C. Eleanor and Mabel van Alstyne Collection 2163, 2164 Galloping animals seemed more popular with older children, while the very young felt safer with the static figures. Deer and rabbit, c. 1890

2164

Leavenworth, Kansas, was the home of the important Parker Carnival Supply Company. Riverside, Rhode Island; Delphos, Ohio; and Germantown, Pennsylvania, each supported a company, while in North Tonawanda two manufacturers of carrousel equipment thrived as a result of the town's unique position in the field. Chicago, Milwaukee, and New York were also centers of merry-go-round activity, as most carvers of this type of work were found in large metropolitan areas. Some makers of carrousel figures were found in the smaller towns where amusement parks were built.

Carrousel animals and circus-wagon figures were related; both supplied the carnival atmosphere, yet there were some differences. On the wagons the figures formed an integral part of the overall decorative theme; the focal points were accentuated in high relief, a contrast to the low-keyed scrollwork. The figures were rarely free-standing or carved in the round. Their backs were flattened so that they could be attached to the wagon sides or to panels. This is the reason for many of the static poses, which were planned as part of an architectonic arrangement with strict spatial limitations. Carrousel figures, on the other hand, were independently carved, since each unit—horse, lion, giraffe, goat, or other animal—was intended for a separate rider. The animal could be viewed from all sides and could be removed without disturbing the surrounding facade. The fast-moving platform provided a forward thrust that determined the action of the animals. Figures in static poses were meant for young children, who were strapped into position. The other figures, usually on the outer rim of the platform, were designed for more daring riders, and the brass ring also attracted older children to the outside positions. In later years, the up-and-down action of the animals provided an extra thrill.

Softwoods, especially white and yellow pine, were most suitable for the carrousel animals. Pine was easily worked, and greater speed of execution meant the figures could be produced quickly in great numbers. Little sanding or polishing was necessary in the detailing of the head, mane, and tail portions. The rounded areas of the body which required sanding were turned over to assistants and apprentices. Finally, the figure was ready for

painting and gilding. These carrousel animals received the same bright-colored treatment as the circus wagons. Frequent refurbishing was necessary to maintain their attractiveness, and often much of the original intention of the artist was obscured.

In the shops where most of this work was done, the carvers worked anonymously. Occasionally, the name of the artist is known, either because of his reputation or from extant billing records. Charles Louff, working in Riverside, Rhode Island, made a name for himself, starting about 1880. Louff carved a number of horses and other animals, including lions, panthers, goats, pigs, deer, and rabbits. They were vigorously executed and notable for detailing. His handling of a horse's mane and tail deviated from the regular grooved hairlines. He introduced locks of hair which curled in various directions, giving each animal an unusual Baroque look. Saddles and blankets also had fancifully carved border designs. Instead of the stereotyped horse in action, with extended forelegs, Louff varied the attitudes to obtain greater originality. He introduced a pair of birds hanging on the hind part of the horse as though the rider were just returning from the chase. In all, Louff's animals were well conceived, realistic, and appropriate to their purpose and function. When removed from carrousel platforms and placed in collections of folk art, they become works of art in their own right.

Bob Crandle, a wood-carver with a small factory on Third Avenue at Thirtieth Street in New York, specialized in hobbyhorses, velocipedes, and merry-go-round horses. The horse bodies were made from large pine-tree trunks, while the limbs were carved separately and doweled into position. Painting produced a variety of equine figures; some were spotted to look like piebald horses and pintos, or even striped to look like zebras. Crandle also carved some lions and giraffes.

The horse was by far the most popular carrousel animal. It was treated in a variety of colorings to imitate the pinto, sorrel, palomino or the spotted white charger, a favorite among young riders. Lions, tigers, giraffes, dogs, roosters, ostriches, and many other exotic members of the menagerie appeared on the colorful carrousels.

2165

2166

2167

2168

608

2169

2165–2172 *The galloping steed was the carrousel's most popular animal, even though some of the more dangerous animals like lions and tigers attracted the daring youngsters. Stirrups were provided, but two- and three-year-olds had to be hoisted into their saddles by parents, who stood alongside. American carrousels with revolving platforms first appeared in 1879. Made in North Tonawanda, New York, between 1880 and 1900*

2170

2172

2171

2173

2174

2173 *Pair of walking panthers yoked together, c. 1890* **2174–2175** *Carrousel goats Louff of Rhode Island. His animal figures were boldly conceived and vigorously carved, suggesting intense liveliness* **2176** *Carrousel whippet; harness treatment provides opportunity for decoration and gilding*

2175

2176

2177

2178

612

2179

2177, 2178 *Carrousel horses, late nineteenth century. Photographs courtesy The Smithsonian Institution, Washington, D.C. Eleanor and Mabel van Alstyne Collection* 2179 *Carrousel pig from Newport, Rhode Island* 2180 *Carrousel rooster from Vermont, c. 1875–1900* 2181 *Carrousel giraffe from Riverside, Rhode Island, c. 1888* 2182 *Carrousel dog by Charles Louff, c. 1880*

2180

2181

2182

2183

2184

2185

2186

2183–2190 *The gay carnival spirit of the carrousel found expression not only in the dynamic action of galloping horses and other animals but in the decorative headpieces used for adornment on the merry-go-round structure, benches, and chariots. Horses' heads,* **2185** *and* **2190,** *are all that survive from full figures. The lions' heads,* **2183, 2186,** *and* **2188,** *were popular architectonic devices whose counterparts are to be found in the work of the figurehead carvers as well.*

2187

2188

Occasionally the forms of other animals were introduced, as in the wolf's head, in **2189,** obviously a derivative from historic ornament. All these were products of the Parker Carnival Supply Company, made about 1890 at Leavenworth, Kansas. The carrousel horse, **2184,** is the work of Charles Louff of Riverside, Rhode Island. It is distinguished from the average run of figures by such spirited and extravagant mannerisms as the tilt of the head, the placement of the horse's legs, the Baroque treatment of the mane, and the decorations on blanket and saddle. All these details, carefully studied and well executed, add to the animation and exuberance of the animal and to the over-all effect

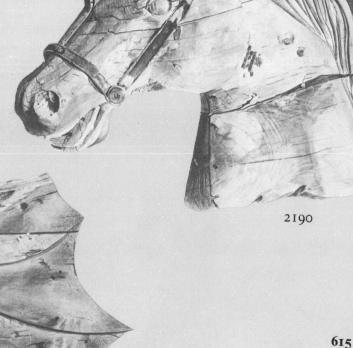

2190

2189

2191

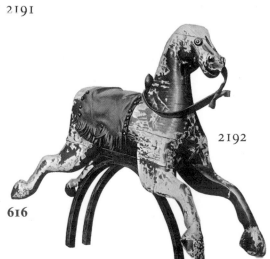

2192

616

2191 The Hobby Horse *was painted about 1840 by an unknown artist in Massachusetts. National Gallery of Art, Washington, D.C. Gift of Edgar William and Bernice Chrysler Garbisch* **2192** *Semicircular hoops provide unusual base for this hobbyhorse* **2193** *Leather horse and rider, c. 1880* **2194** *Musician nods his head and moves his bow in mechanical music box, c. 1890*

Playthings & Pastimes

2193

2194

CHILDREN'S TOYS mirror the tastes and trends of their times, and the toys of the early Colonial days in turn reflect the unfrivolous nature of that period. Very often there were no toys at all and imagination served to turn sticks and stones into games; children who lived along the seashore played with shells and pebbles. By the end of the seventeenth century, some English toys were being imported, but they were available to only a small fraction of the population. For the most part the early settlers fashioned crude playthings out of pine, oak, maple, and cherry wood from the forest.

The rocking horse, or hobbyhorse, was the most popular form of amusement for all children. Its design and construction presented a real challenge to the artisan—an opportunity to demonstrate imagination in contriving it from a single plank or shaping it sculpturally. Collectively, a group of hobbyhorses reveals the wide range of skills found among amateur craftsmen. The back and saddle of the horse

required clever design for comfortable seating and the runners had to be sturdy enough for constant rocking over long periods. Realism in equine features was a matter of the toymaker's patience and ability; the lack of it in cruder models certainly did not hinder the child's fun. The plank forms, thin and elongated in their more economical construction, had the universal appeal of all primitive things. The more elaborate, full-bodied shapes approach carrousel figures of a later day and represent the handiwork of skilled carvers rather than amateur craftsmen. Hobbyhorses were forthright examples of folk carving and ingenuity, from the leather ears tacked into position to the genuine horsehair tails.

In New England villages the making of toys became a sideline for carvers and carpenters. In Pennsylvania German counties, where toymaking descended from the distinctive wood carving of the homeland, there was an abundance of charming miniatures—animals, birds, and other figures. Noah's Ark, with its full complement of paired birds and beasts, was

2195

2196

2197

particulary attractive to children. In addition there were the traditional Christmas decorations—the crêche and nativity scenes. Celebrated itinerants included the German carvers Wilhelm Schimmel and Aaron Mountz (often spelled Mounts) and the Swiss George Huguenin. Although Schimmel was especially noted for his birds, his most elaborate creation was the Garden of Eden, of which he made a number of copies. Here he stood Adam and Eve in the shade of a tree, surrounded them with a variety of animals, and enclosed the whole ensemble within a picket fence. He covered all this with heavy coats of whatever paint was available at the farmhouse, most often a barn red.

The wooden figures, although faithfully executed, still had one drawback: they lacked the animation so necessary to a child's sense of play. Out of this urgent need there developed other wooden toys, articulated with moving parts and mechanical arrangements of the simplest sort. Whirligigs, tall, attenuated figures with arms pivoted through the shoulders, revolved about a central axis. Windmills were built in miniature and mounted on boards to spin freely when the wind reached sufficient velocity. Other mechanical contrivances involved watermills with overshot wheels. Still another was a figure balanced on a horizontal bar actuated by a crank handle. Again, the Pennsylvania Germans devised all manner of revolving mechanisms—music boxes with many figures mounted on a spinning platform, stamping mills in which hammers pounded and clattered, and figures whirling around a maypole, all colorfully designed and attractively painted. Carved wooden pieces in which balls were imprisoned within bars constituted an exercise for the whittler's own amusement. Often the tour-de-force was a wooden chain of many links.

The vast variety of wooden toys included sets of miniature furniture with which to equip an entire dollhouse. There were chairs, tables, benches, stools, chests, beds, lowboys, and highboys. Some of these pieces, especially those made by a cabinetmaker for his children, are our finest examples of diminutive woodworking. Welsh dressers and corner cabinets provided display pieces in which to show off the child's precious bits of miniature china and porcelain. An important addition to doll equipment was an American creation: the doll carriage. It came in every possible style and size and was usually a sideline of baby-carriage makers. Later on, in the second half of the nineteenth century, reed and wicker bodies replaced the wooden ones, which had been heavier and sturdier. The doll carriage was subjected to constant use and frequently handed down.

As tin toys followed those made of wood, in about 1840, a new realm opened up for the toy makers. Dies could easily stamp out all shapes and forms, which could then be crimped together at the seams for extra strength and rigidity. Mechanical playthings, a constant source of amusement for children, now also gained a new dimension. Though simple actions had been known as early as 1825, the windup, or clockwork, toys with spring action came in with the popular wave of tin toys. These mechanisms could be installed to make a figure dance a jig, play an instrument, or—in the case of dolls—simply walk. They could produce locomotion in steam engines, paddle-wheelers, and fire trucks. Windup toys included capering clowns, music boxes, revolving tables on which monkeys danced, and a thousand and one novelties ideally suited to tin because of its lightness and the low cost of its manufacture. The present scarcity of tin toys from the seventies and eighties is incomprehensible when one remembers the record-breaking output of the toy makers in their heyday. One single manufacturer is known to have produced forty million tin toys annually in the 1870s.

Fortunately for today's collectors, the cast-iron variety, which came in a bit later than tin, had a better chance for survival. Although

2195–2200 *Design, construction, and rocker action vary greatly. Very low horses, sometimes called rocking chairs, are for tiny tots under two. The primitive horse, 2198, was made in Minnesota, 1902. The horse and rider, 2200, is only a toy*

2198

2199

2200

2201

2202

2203

2204

620

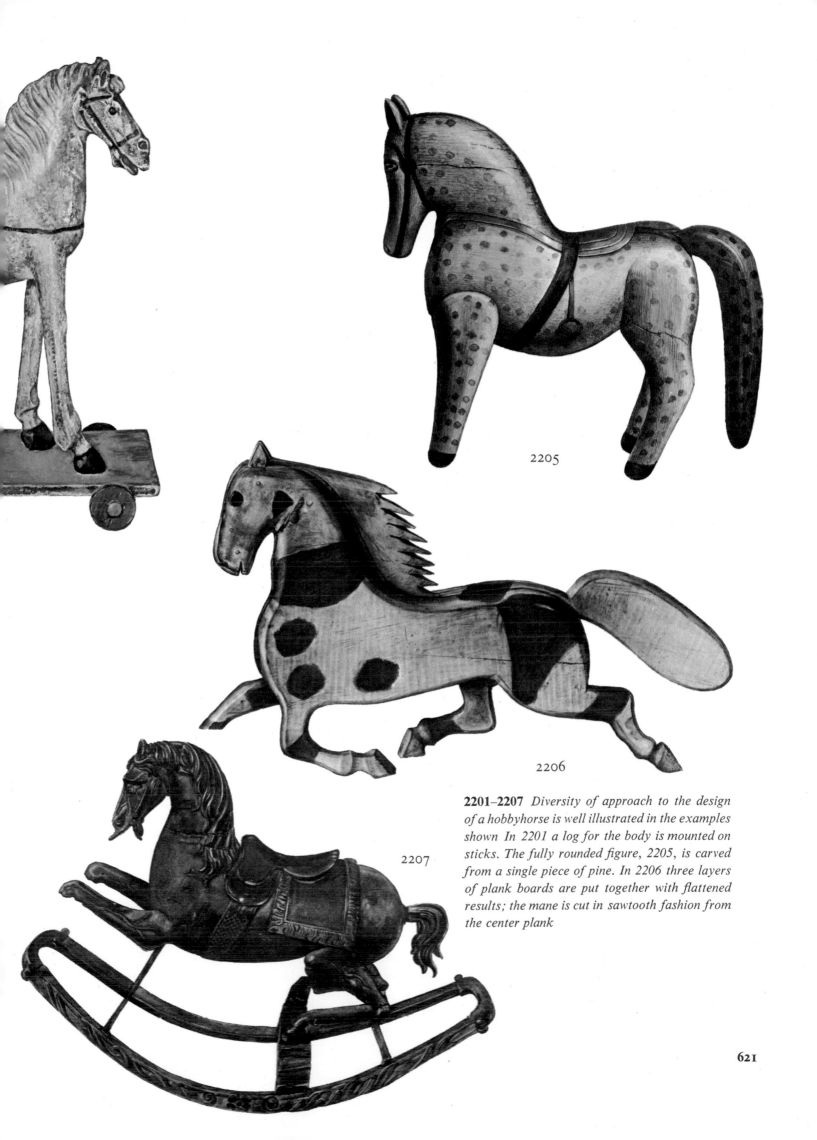

2205

2206

2207

2201–2207 *Diversity of approach to the design of a hobbyhorse is well illustrated in the examples shown In 2201 a log for the body is mounted on sticks. The fully rounded figure, 2205, is carved from a single piece of pine. In 2206 three layers of plank boards are put together with flattened results; the mane is cut in sawtooth fashion from the center plank*

2208   2209   2210

2208 Whirligig, Sailor Jack, made in the eighteenth century 2209 Wooden toy, hand operated, c. 1800 2210 Bouncing jack made of oak, c. 1800–1830 2211 Lumberjack carving of pine and oak, c. 1885 2212 Wooden dachshund with movable joints, c. 1880 2213 Wooden toy with revolving horses and riders 2214 Windup toy of wood and cast iron in which boxers box 2215 Building a Noah's Ark was an exercise in shaping many wooden animals

2211   2212

2213

2214

cast-iron toys were indeed more solid, windup mechanisms were not suited to the heavier material, and vehicles equipped with wheels or rollers had to be pulled along by the child. In this category were the bell toys, which so delighted young children. The bell device was most often attached to the axle of a cart or horse-drawn wagon and the bell chimed when the toy was in motion. Cast-iron pots, pans, and skillets were favored by young girls. Together with a miniature stove, these vessels completed a girl's kitchen equipment and could be used for baking cakes and cookies.

2215

623

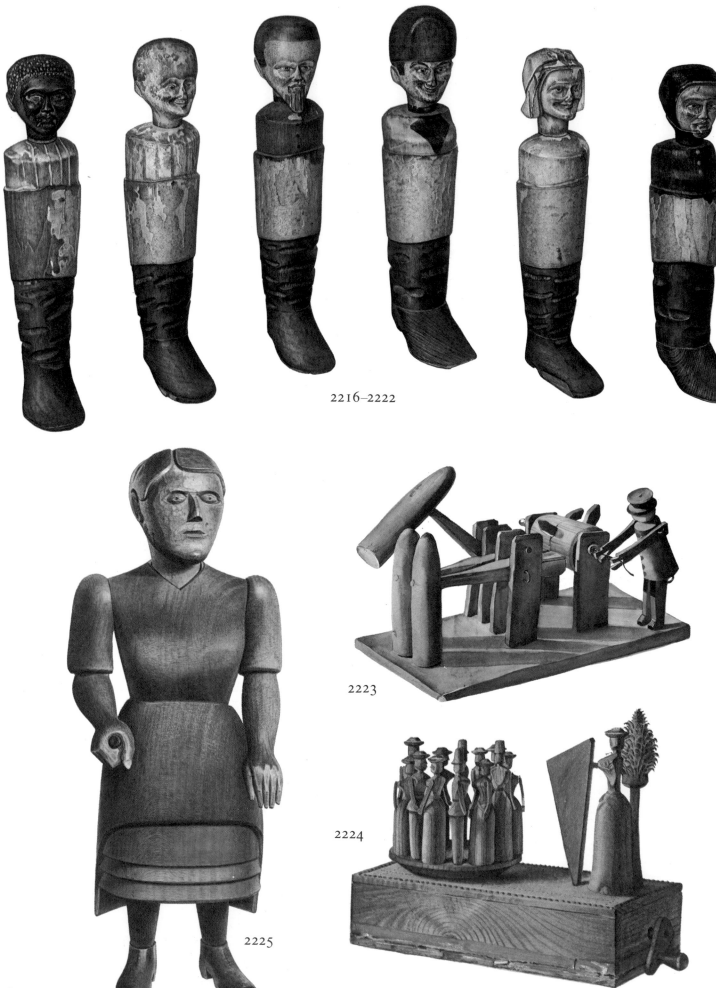

2216–2222

2223

2224

2225

624

2226   2227   2228

The perennial favorites for boys were transportation models, which the toy makers built with endless ingenuity. The early prototypes of vehicles were jigsawed of wood and often had lithographs pasted over the flat surfaces to lend color and interest. With the advent of new methods and materials everything was possible: farm wagons and circus wagons, sailing vessels and steamboats, fire engines and delivery trucks, trolley cars and trains; a cow catcher heading a locomotive was a distinctly American feature. Trains and locomotives were eventually extended to an entire railway system of tunnels, bridges, depots, switches, and every other known accessory which could be made in miniature.

2216–2222 *Set of ninepins probably carved by a settler in the Pennsylvania German region, midnineteenth century* **2223, 2224** *Toy stamping mill of trip-hammers and revolving mannequins in music box. Made in Pennsylvania, c. 1840* **2225** *Carved wooden housewife with movable joints* **2226–2228** *Wooden costumed figures* **2229** *Carved statue of farm couple*

2229

2231

2230

2232

2233

2230–2236 *The saga of American transportation, at a time when great progress was being made in every direction, is reflected in a cavalcade of vehicular toys fashioned of wood, cast iron, and tin. The progression starts with the team of oxen, 2230, and the covered wagon, 2231, followed by the fire engine, 2232, the cast-iron train set, 2233, the tin omnibus, 2234, and the tin steamboat side-wheeler, 2236. Typical of cast-iron bell toys is the Pony Bell Ringer, 2235. Figures 2230 and 2235 from photographs*

2234

2235

2236

627

2237

2238

2239

2240

2241

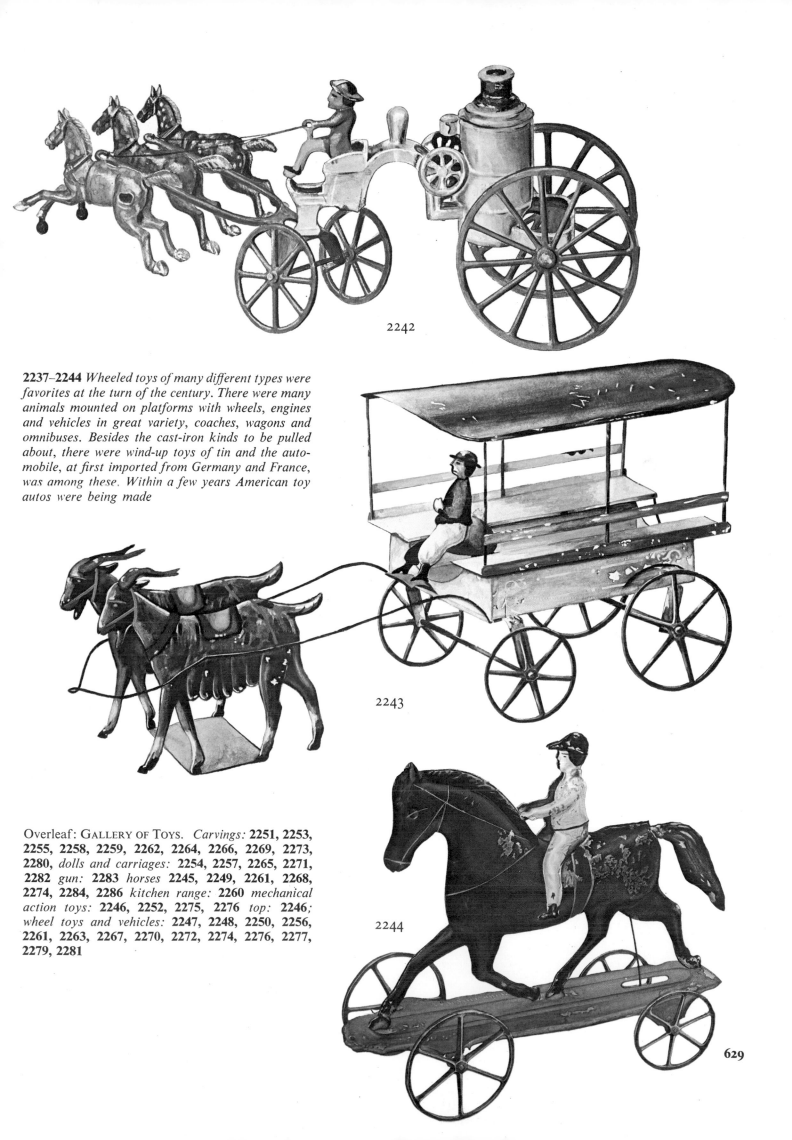

2242

2237–2244 *Wheeled toys of many different types were favorites at the turn of the century. There were many animals mounted on platforms with wheels, engines and vehicles in great variety, coaches, wagons and omnibuses. Besides the cast-iron kinds to be pulled about, there were wind-up toys of tin and the automobile, at first imported from Germany and France, was among these. Within a few years American toy autos were being made*

2243

Overleaf: GALLERY OF TOYS. *Carvings:* **2251, 2253, 2255, 2258, 2259, 2262, 2264, 2266, 2269, 2273, 2280,** *dolls and carriages:* **2254, 2257, 2265, 2271, 2282** *gun:* **2283** *horses* **2245, 2249, 2261, 2268, 2274, 2284, 2286** *kitchen range:* **2260** *mechanical action toys:* **2246, 2252, 2275, 2276** *top:* **2246;** *wheel toys and vehicles:* **2247, 2248, 2250, 2256, 2261, 2263, 2267, 2270, 2272, 2274, 2276, 2277, 2279, 2281**

2244

629

2245

2246

2247

2248

2253

2254

2255

2256

2261

2262

2263

2264

2269

2270

2271

2272

2277

2278

2279

2280

2249

2250

2251

2252

2257

2258

2259

2260

2265

2266

2267

2268

2273

2274

2275

2276

2281

2282

2283

2284

2285

2286

631

2287

2288–2292

Dolls, Puppets

& Marionettes

2293

DOLLS, PUPPETS, and marionettes have always figured largely in the child's world of fantasy. Fortunately, their size and shape have not mattered, for in the early days of the Colonies the homemade dolls were crude indeed. One of the earliest, which was called—because of the obvious similarity—a bedpost doll, was simply a rounded stick with a face painted on it. In some regions children learned from friendly Indian tribes how to make simple puppets out of buckskin. But the universal favorites, on the farm and in the city, were rag dolls, which could be made by anybody who

2287 *Marionette Chinaman made to be operated by strings from a position above the stage. Head carved of black walnut and painted, costume of silk with rhinestone buttons, and papier-maché ball. Made by puppeteer Oliver Lano, c. 1870* **2288–2292** *Painted puppet heads of carved walnut. Wigs were made of fur and wool by Oliver Lano, c. 1870* **2293** *Hand puppet, Judy, has stick in the body to hold up head. Painted wooden face and hands, velvet cap, and cotton clothing, c. 1870*

owned an extra bit of cloth; often a clothespin was used for the body. In an era of make-do they became cherished possessions.

The popularity of rag dolls eventually led to the manufacture of dolls in quantity. The pattern was made by stamping or printing a design on two separate pieces of cloth, one for the front and the other for the back. These were then cut out, sewn together, and stuffed.

Rag dolls were dressed in pieces of calico, muslin, linen, or silk left over from a dress or an appliqué bedspread. Occasionally a doll might be clad in Quaker costume, but on the whole regional dress was not in evidence. There were, however, marked variations in doll construction, with cornhusks and nuthead dolls prevailing in rural areas.

Gradually dolls became more elaborate. The importation of papier-maché heads started in the early nineteenth century. These were mounted on canvas, linen, or kid bodies stuffed with sawdust. China heads from Austria and Germany came next, followed by wax heads from England. Unclothed dolls' bodies could be bought and costumed to suit the current taste. Of even greater interest to the ladies were the so-called milliners' models, fashion replicas sent from abroad as an advance showing of the new styles.

Innovations constantly appeared on the doll market. In the 1870s a Yankee inventor named Joel Ellis came up with the mortise-and-tenon joint, by which wooden pieces could be inserted and fastened, or made movable. The practicability of these for doll construction led Ellis to the formation of a Vermont company for the manufacture of dolls that could assume all sorts of odd positions and perform acrobatic stunts. His success inspired the invention of the ball-and-socket joint for doll movements and many other improvements. After the walking doll came the talking doll, a by-product of Thomas Edison's work on the phonograph.

Puppets and marionettes have followed a very different pattern, since they are completely handmade, from the fashioning of the heads and facial expressions to the articulation of the figures and their costuming. Puppeteers make a clear distinction that sometimes comes as a surprise to the layman. In the true meaning, puppets are manipulated directly by hand, or sometimes with a stick from underneath; marionettes are controlled by strings or wires from above. The puppeteer often conceives, writes, and directs the play, designs the stage and costumes, and creates all the sets and stage appurtenances in his own workshop. The miniature theater offers a rare form of self-expression in which artist, craftsman, stage director, and actor are combined in a single personality.

The lineage of the puppet show may be traced to ancient times in Rome, Greece, Egypt, and India, where costumed figures and effigies were carried in awe-inspiring religious processionals and on festive occasions. During the Middle Ages, puppets played their roles in miracle and Passion plays. As the repertory broadened they started to appear in secular entertainment, taking on native forms in different countries. In France the favorites were called Guignol and Polichinelle. In England and America we know them as Punch and Judy. The English Punch entertained his audiences by telling of his marital troubles with Judy and by his impertinent antics. The portraits of Punch and his fellow players are so excellent that the characters seem almost human and have served as models for many a subsequent play. As W. H. Chesson expressed it, Punch is made "a goggling miscreant, whose hump is a rigid and misplaced tail and whose military hat, above a crustacean face, completes a rather melancholy effect of mania." Almost a hundred years ago this figure, like that of the wooden Indian, stood outside many tobacconist shops, his big nose suggesting the fragrance of cheroots and the spice of snuff. While Punch was the perennial villain, low-browed, vile, and murderous, Judy was pictured as a beauty, the continual butt of her husband's machinations and anger. Cruikshank, the English illustrator, has given us a fine set of twenty-four watercolor drawings of Punch and Judy.

There have been few improvements in the technique of the puppet theater since Punch began his travels in England, almost three centuries ago. The methods of puppetry have a basic simplicity and honesty which do not encourage innovation. The stage is formed within a portable wooden framework which is covered with cloth or decorated alfresco. At the bottom edge of the stage opening, which generally comes just above the puppeteer's head, is a projecting shelf on which the properties may be placed. Sometimes there is a flap below the main opening out of which the devil may make a surprise appearance. Scenery is painted simply on cloth drops or board cutouts; for the purpose of the average Punch play a garden or any scene will serve. Furniture is not generally used. The gallows are set up by pegging the base of the gibbet into a hole in the shelf.

The puppets are hung upside down by loops in their skirts on a row of hooks inside the booth. The puppeteer plunges his hand into the opening of the hollow costume, slips his index finger into the neck of the puppet, his thumb into one arm and his second finger into the other, and brings the figure onstage right side up. It is held at arm's length over his head. Punch is always on the right hand and the other characters change on the left hand while Punch holds the attention of the audience. Sometimes extras, an army or a mob, are held up on a forked stick.

The roving puppeteers who delighted children on street corners or village greens in seven-teenth-century England, or at country fairs or in taverns of New England two centuries later, had a universal appeal to people of all ages. Nathaniel Hawthorne, thrilled by such a performance, wrote in 1838: "After supper, as the sun was setting, a man passed by the tavern door with a hand-organ, connected with which was a row of figures, such as dancers, pirouetting and twining, a lady playing on a piano, soldiers . . . all these keeping time to the lively or slow tunes of the organ. He had come over the high, solitary mountains where for miles there could hardly be a soul to watch his players and hear his music."

The marionette makers have a long tradition of creativity; many families engaged in puppetry have handed down their knowledge and experience for generations. One such outstanding group was the Lano family, whose forebears had trundled puppet shows about the streets of Milan in a handbarrow. Oliver Lano, the son of Alberto Lano, came to the United States in 1825. In their heyday the American Lano puppets traveled in the frontier country playing in obscure places, often with hastily improvised settings and impromptu programs. Teamed with circuses and medicine shows, puppet plays were only one number on a variety bill. Casual, leisurely, and unpretentious, the Lano puppets were fairly typical of wandering shows before the days of organized theater. Like other small shows on the frontier scene, they were welcomed in remote places as a great event. Their repertory included many scripts of the Punch and Judy variety as well as performances about David and Goliath, Robinson Crusoe, and other perennials. The Lano characters are known as fine examples of dramatic caricature. Their facial expressions were deeply carved for extreme emphasis, then painted with great imagination. Erwin Christensen, in his book *Early American Wood Carving*, describes them as follows:

2294

2295

2296

The judge who presides over Punch's trial for his life is truly menacing in his ghostlike pallor, and the Devil himself glows with his red cheeks and green eyes reflecting the tortures of hell. For color is as varied as shape, and both together are used with gusto. One looks in wonder at these raucous characters, broadly grinning, or open-eyed, teeth showing and chins pushed forward as if prepared for a savage attack. Devices like the shoe-button eye are in the tradition of the craft itself.

Carving and painting merged to produce an effect of grotesque fantasy well suited to slapstick comedy.

The puppeteer puts his heart and soul into carving the facial features of his puppets; the face symbolizes the entire character. Regardless of the puppets' actions, one sees only the helpless look of the heroine or the snarl of the villain. In the final analysis, it was the well-defined facial structure, fashioned with economy, that spelled success for the puppeteer.

2294–2299 *Marionettes as various characters in plays by the Lano family, well-known puppeteers, c. 1870. The Cannibal is shown in 2297, and the Sultan's Choice, a fan dancer, in 2299* **2300, 2301** *Puppets Punch and Judy, made by the Lano family, c. 1880*

2297

2298

2299

2300

2301

2302

2303

2304

2305

2306

2307

2302-2309 *Costumed dolls reflect the mood and manner of a particular era and were dressed according to the materials available, usually dressmaking remnants. Limbs were mostly cotton sewn together and stuffed, sometimes containing sticks to make them rigid, c. 1850–90*

2308

2309

2310

2311

2312

640

2313

2314

2315

2316

2317

Overleaf: GALLERY OF DOLLS AND PUPPETS. *Most of the examples shown may be classified as costume dolls whether they are clad in rags or silks and whether or not they are stuffed. Heads are made of muslin, yarn, wax, wood, or bisque. Others include Indian dolls:* **2351, 2365;** *male dolls:* **2330, 2347** *(General Grant);* **2352, 2358;** *manikins:* **2341, 2554** *(Indian); marionette:* **2325;** *puppets:* **2322, 2344** *(witch lantern),* **2346, 2349 2350, 2356, 2361, 2364, 2366;** *undressed:* **2334**

2310–2312 *The doll maker exercised much ingenuity in the construction of head and face when imported wax or bisque heads were unavailable. Cornhusks, nutheads, papier-maché, woven yarn, and stuffed cottons were a few of the materials pressed into service* **2313, 2314** *Pair of Indian dolls with carved wooden heads, stuffed bodies, and buckskin costumes. Made by Marie Rose of the Montana Cree Reservation* **2315** *Rag doll Tilly, made about 1880* **2316** *Negro doll with carved wooden head and stuffed body, made about 1870* **2317** *Hand-painted doll's cradle, made in Pennsylvania, c. 1780*

2318   2319   2320   2321   2322   2323

2330   2331   2332   2333   2334   2335   2336

2344   2345   2346   2347   2348   2349

2356   2357   2358   2359   2360   2361   2362

2324   2325   2326   2327   2328   2329

2337   2338   2339   2340   2341   2342   2343

2350   2351   2352   2353   2354   2355

2363   2364   2365   2366   2367   2368   2369

2370

644

A Penny Saved....

2371

THRIFT WAS among the virtues that nineteenth-century parents tried to instill in their children. Every primer and Bible tract emphasized the value of saving a penny: "Resolve not to be poor; whatever you have, spend less and save more." "It is saving, not getting, that is the mother of riches," Benjamin Franklin had put it earlier. Proverbs and sermons of thrift at home or in Bible school were not entirely effective, however. It took the inventiveness of the small iron foundries to hit

2370 *Cast-iron and polychromed Uncle Sam mechanical bank made its debut shortly after the Centennial Exhibition. It became one of the most popular toy banks of its day* **2371** *A penny deposited brought the promise of action and a faint bark from the Speaking Dog bank, patented in 1885*

on a method of combining thrift with fun. Between 1850 and 1910, millions of mechanical banks were made by a handful of foundries.

Large copper pieces were first issued by the government in 1793; this led to improvised forms of the piggy bank made from gourds, clay, seashells, and some even whittled from wood. Such contrivances were followed by glass and china banks in a variety of shapes— houses, chickens, ducks, turkeys, wild and tame animals, public characters, and historic landmarks, including Plymouth Rock and the Liberty Bell.

By 1857, when the minting of large copper pennies was discontinued, manufacturers turned to the production of painted tin banks that looked like churches, gabled houses, drums, and bandboxes.

Just after the Civil War the first iron banks appeared. They were modeled after the square bank buildings, with a cupola and a "Savings Bank" inscription over the door. This plain bank building, unfortunately, offered little opportunity for novelty. Then the insertion of a simple spring action brought life into the still bank. Patent applications for the new designs have provided us with a record of the various types of mechanical banks. From about 1870, the intricate movements became increasingly popular, reaching a peak in sales before the close of the century. A single penny deposited in the slot brought a ticket of admission—a sideshow, a bit of amusement enjoyed by children and adults alike. The toy soldiers bowed, the mule kicked his heels, and the eagle flapped its wings. This approach to thrift proved more effective than stern admonitions

and moralizing maxims.

Less than a dozen firms produced these mechanical banks. A leader among them was the J. & E. Stevens Company, Cromwell, Connecticut, whose 1873 catalogue listed about two dozen distinct patterns. Other companies were located in Philadelphia and Lancaster, Pennsylvania; Kenton, Ohio; and Buffalo, New York. As each new volume or bit of research on this subject is completed, the total number of patterns increases. The latest count records about six hundred designs. The banks were manufactured in forms that made up a veritable Noah's Ark, complete with frogs, turtles, rabbits, owls, pigs, horses, elephants, and lions. The American eagle feeding its young was a favorite. Others included a Punch and Judy theater, baseball batter and battery, the Old Woman Who Lived in the Shoe, a bowling alley, ping-pong players, fortunetellers, wood-choppers, and the like. Comic situations also had appeal: a boy being thrown by his mule or turning a somersault.

Current events played their part in influencing the choice of subjects. At the time of fairs and celebrations, such forms as Uncle Sam, the Liberty Bell, and Independence Hall were produced by different foundries. Novelties were issued for special occasions, such as the Columbian World's Fair in 1892 and the Pan-American Exposition in 1901.

Although hardly an expression of folk art, the mechanical banks represent another field in which the patternmaker, molder, and colorist combined their talents to create articles of mass appeal.

2372

2373

2374

648

2375

2376

2377

2372 *Spring action in the gun of William Tell sent the penny flying at the apple on the boy's head, 1896* 2373 *Black Sambo characters were a product of the 1880s* 2374 *For a penny the mule cart tipped upward, sending the mule into midair* 2375 *Growing interest in baseball made this Dark Town Battery a favorite in its day, 1888* 2376 *A coin is placed on the clown's hand, the lever is pressed in the back, and presto, the coin is swallowed* 2377 *A cannon shoots the coin into the pylon of this Artillery Bank, 1892*

2378

2379

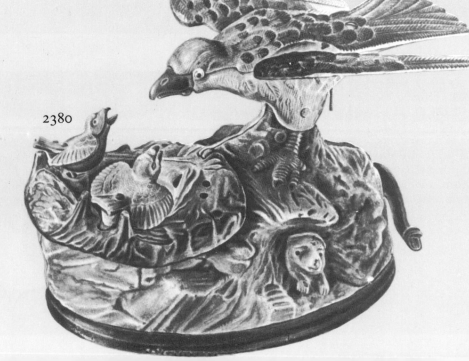

2380

2381

2382

2383

2378 *The monkey throws the coins right into the lion's mouth every time* 2379 *Hod carrier and bricklayer supply the simple action in this mechanical bank* 2380 *As the mother eagle dropped her coin into the waiting young beaks she flapped her wings and there was a chirp from within* 2381 *Teddy and the Bear celebrated an incident in one of Roosevelt's hunting expeditions. As the coin is shot into the tree trunk a bear's head pops up* 2382 *Bank titled "Always Did 'Spise a Mule" rears hind legs as sitter falls forward in astonishment* 2383 *Rooster bank is activated by lever in tail, causing head to raise and crow while coin is dropped into slot, c. 1875*

2384

2385

2384 *Jonah banks his coins in the wide-open mouth of the whale, 1888* **2385** *When the right forefoot is pressed, the frog's mouth opens wide to receive coin, 1872* **2386** *The bear and hunter, in many versions, shoot the coin into a pouch for safekeeping, c. 1895* **2387** *After coin deposit mule swings a-round to kick over watching boy (see 2382)* **2388** *Organ Bank plays a tune as monkey doffs his hat and drops coin into slot* **2389** *Trick Dog jumps through the hoop and lands coin in the barrel*

2386

2387

2388

2389

ORGAN BANK

TRICK DOG

654

2390

2391

2392

2393

2394

2395

2390 *"Still banks" rely more upon design than action. The Liberty Bell bank appeared at the time of the Philadelphia Centennial* **2391** *The Statue of Liberty obliges with a peal when a penny is deposited, c. 1885* **2392** *Independence Hall bank appeared just before the Centennial of 1876* **2393** *Santa Claus obligingly dropped his penny into the Christmas chimney* **2394** *Many coin banks were modeled on the architectural forms of the bank building* **2395** *Corpulent receiver of coins was called the Tammany Bank*

2396

2397

656

2398

2399

2400

2401

2402

2396 *The swinging acrobat provides the action in this mechanical bank, c. 1875* 2397 *Punch and Judy bank provides action in the stage setting, 1884* 2398 *Circus Elephant performs as follows: coin is placed between rings at lower right, ball held by acrobat at left is pulled back, clown turns at waist, and elephant's trunk flicks coin into slot, 1882* 2399 *Figure in bank building turns to make deposit* 2400 *Trick Pony takes coin in his mouth and bends his head to drop it into feedbox* 2401 *The clown seated on a globe does a turn as coin is placed into*

slot 2402 *The miser holding bills waves his arms in this bank of very limited action, c. 1875*

Overleaf: GALLERY OF COIN BANKS. *Animals and birds:* **2403, 2408, 2412, 2418, 2423, 2424, 2426, 2429, 2430;** *buildings:* **2407, 2410, 2413, 2414, 2417, 2428, 2431, 2435, 2438;** *mechanical action banks:* **2404, 2406, 2409, 2415, 2416, 2419–2422, 2427, 2432, 2433, 2436, 2437;** *patriotic:* **2405, 2434.** *From photographs except 2405, 2407, 2409–2411, 2413–15, 2417, 2421, 2424–26, 2428–30, 2432, 2434, 2435, 2438*

657

2403

2404

2405

2406

2411

2412

2413

2414

2419

2420

2421

2422

2427

2428

2429

2430

2435

2407

2408

2409

2410

2415

2416

2417

2418

2423

2424

2425

2426

2431

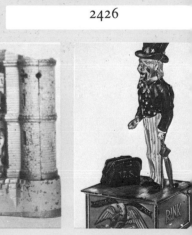

2432

2433

2434

Hudson River Valley, Sunset, *painted c. 1850 by Thomas Chambers. Little is known about the artist except that he was born in England in 1808 and came to the United States in 1832. Primarily a painter of marine views, landscapes, and portraits, he lived and worked for long periods in New York, Boston, and Albany. There are no records of his later career, or of the place and date of his death. Many of his landscapes are said to have been inspired by engraved views of American scenery similar to those done after the watercolor paintings of William H. Bartlett. Another version of this scene, with changes in the river boats, indicates some duplication in his dozen works so far identified. National Gallery of Art, Washington, D.C. Gift of Edgar William and Bernice Chrysler Garbisch*

BOOK
SIX

Across the Nation

BOOK SIX: *Across the Nation*

2439

2439 The Conestoga wagon, so called because it originated in the Conestoga Valley of Lancaster County, Pennsylvania, was a landmark achievement in pure American utilitarian design. It was ruggedly constructed to withstand the strain of overland travel and to carry several tons' cargo in addition to the large families of its owners. The ingeniously contrived curved wagon bed prevented cargo from rolling and spilling when traveling the uphill terrain of the Alleghenies or when fording rivers en route. Strictly functional in every detail, the few places where native crafts could find expression were in the toolbox lids of wrought-iron hardware, hinges and hasps, or the decorated brake shoes. As generations of German families pushed westward, starting as early as 1755, the familiar Conestoga became the symbol of the frontier settler seeking to make his fortune in America's unconquered regions

2440 Carved wooden bag stamp used to identify a farmer's homespun grain bag at the miller's **2441** Egg cup of turned wood made and decorated by G. Lehn, a retired farmer. Late nineteenth century

From the Rhineland to Penn's Land

2440

THE PROMISE of freedom of worship brought the first immigrants from the German Palatinate to America during the fall of 1682. Through the efforts of William Penn and his Quaker agents for the German Land Company, the wooded regions bordering the Delaware valley and an area hundreds of miles to the west were opened to them for colonization. Here the immigrants could settle, free from endless war, religious persecution, and excessive taxes. This immigration from Germany grew steadily until the middle of the eighteenth century. In 1738, for example, some nine thousand persons landed in the busy port of Philadelphia.

Many of the new immigrants came over as indentured servants, with contracts to work from two to seven years to repay their passage. Not all, however, were peasants or farm people—some were much-needed artisans and craftsmen such as masons, carpenters, tanners, bakers, butchers, and blacksmiths. The members of this group of Colonists who prospered most were the husbandmen who knew best how to farm the Pennsylvania fields.

The German settlers in America either belonged to the Lutheran and Reformed churches or followed the more austere beliefs of the Anabaptists. Among the latter were the Amish and the Mennonites, called "the plain people," who renounced all worldly frills,

2441

quirks of fashion, and modern inventions. To this day, they wear distinctively plain clothes, shun the automobile, and exclude all superfluous ornament from their simple farmhouses.

With a stubborn tenacity, the Amish and Mennonite pietists resisted any and all outside influences and attempts to assimilate them into American life. They constituted a self-reliant enclave, self-supporting and self-governing, yet never antagonistic to the laws of the land. Their own press published their newspapers and journals in their native German tongue; publishers issued or imported German books and Bibles for use in the schools, and English was all but unknown. As late as 1911, it was necessary to make English compulsory in the public schools of the region. The possible consequences of entertaining a large group almost immune to Americanization were noted early by Benjamin Franklin, who wrote: "Unless the stream of their importation could be turned from this to other Colonies . . . they will soon so outnumber us, that all advantages we have will not (in my opinion) be able to preserve our language."

This never happened, yet the ways and habits of the Pennsylvania Dutch (a misnomer derived from the word *Deutsch*, meaning "German") linger after almost three centuries. It is estimated that about a third of a million people, both here and in Canada, still speak with pronounced traces of the original dialect.

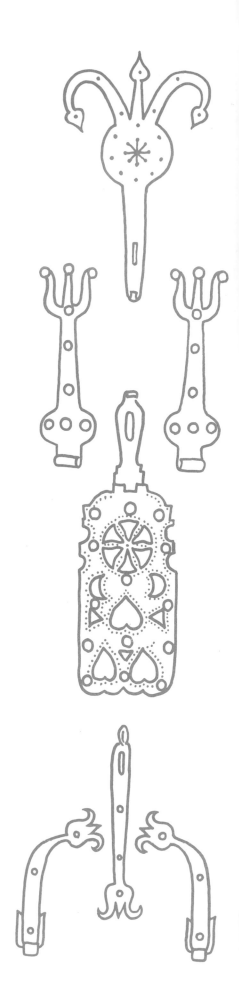

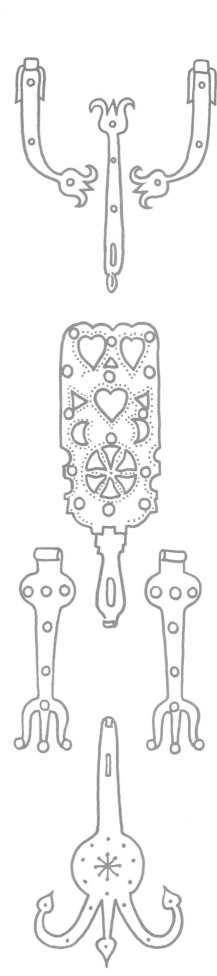

This very insularity has also preserved a heritage in the arts and crafts that is without parallel for originality, purity, and diversity.

In establishing themselves on virgin soil, the transplanted German farmers banded together in groups with artisans in order to furnish all necessary articles, the design of which was rooted in the medieval German culture. When a farmer could not build what he needed, he turned to his brethern. Craftsmen equipped the early settlers with essentials. Thereafter, other skilled workers, such as cabinetmakers, coppersmiths, and silversmiths, added grace and beauty to the simple homesteads.

The decorators and craftsmen of the region were not original designers. They adapted and intelligently applied decorative motifs almost identical to those of the Rhineland Palatinate. They used the unicorn, a fabled symbol of purity, to decorate many fine chests that were crafted in Berks County. The peacock, a symbol of resurrection, appeared on ceramic plates and pottery as well as on *Fraktur* birth and wedding certificates. The tulip, basic to the decorative vocabulary of the region, first bloomed on the Continent at Augsburg in 1554. It was brought into the Western world from Turkey, and its popularity spread thoughout Europe. The tulip became an important decorative motif in southwestern Germany, and subsequently appeared on many fine examples of Pennsylvania German furniture and folk art.

2442

668

2443

2442 *Displayed on the open shelves of this Pennsylvania German pine cupboard of the eighteenth century are earthenware plates, jars, and jugs with slip and sgraffito decoration. Photograph courtesy the Henry Francis du Pont Winterthur Museum, Winterthur, Delaware*

To a Bit of Clay
They Added Beauty

2444

PENNSYLVANIA GERMAN settlers from the Rhine Valley inherited a love for ornamental kitchenware which reflected Old World techniques and traditions. The abundance of native red clay, the endless supply of fuel, and the ease in setting up a kiln were ideally suited to the continuation of their pottery handicrafts.

Directly beneath the rich, fertile soil of eastern Pennsylvania, especially in Montgomery, Bucks, and Berks counties, a good quality of potter's clay was found. Once a potter located a supply, he stripped the top layer of soil to a depth of about six inches in an area

about five by ten feet. The clay was then dug and hauled to a homemade kiln. When one clay pit was exhausted, the potter had no difficulty in finding another close at hand.

Kitchen articles were the first to be fashioned from this clay—plates, pots, bowls, and baking dishes. The potter also produced red roofing tiles, reminiscent of his European homeland, a practice that has continued into the twentieth century. All potters made nests of pots in graded sizes for apple butter and milk; covered earthenware jars for pickles and preserves; mixing bowls, jelly molds and colanders; and handled jugs for cider and vinegar,

2443 *Covered earthenware dish of pierced work required extreme care in the cutting. Such work was often performed by potters who sought to impress their prospective employers with their skill* **2444** *In this sugar bowl the lid has a unique decoration of many-tiered beaded flanges and scrolls* **2445** *Covered jar from southeastern Pennsylvania shows the sgraffito treatment of conventional tulip-and-leaf design. Made in 1830*

2445

which were stoppered with corncob stumps. Many potters turned out red clay teapots, dark-brown coffeepots, cups, thick mugs of quart capacity for ale or spirits, and pitchers in varying sizes. There were enormous platters in oval, round, or octagonal shapes and casseroles with ornamental covers.

Aside from kitchenware, many other household articles were supplied by the potter: washbowls, candlesticks, lamp bases, hot-water bottles, soap dishes, shaving mugs and bowls, vases, flowerpots, and hanging baskets. Smaller objects included inkstands and sanders, toys, pipes, and coin banks. For the most part these were crafted in simple forms and shapes, strictly utilitarian and unadorned. However, when the homemaker wanted something special, "just for fancy," the potter produced his version of fashionable imported Staffordshire mantel ornaments or Bohemian bric-a-brac, such as little figurines, birds, and animals. These were crude and quaint, yet they satisfied the aesthetic standards of those who remembered the earthenware knickknacks of the homeland. These fancy pieces were by no means numerous; at best, they represented a small fraction of the potter's output. They survived because they were given a place of honor in the home.

The most prized pieces of pottery today are the highly original ornamental ware made in the European tradition by a few Pennsylvania potters. Their mastery of ceramic techniques attained a level of artistic excellence difficult to match in the vast field of American folk arts. Presentation pieces were commissioned as gifts for weddings, birthdays, or anniversaries.

Much care was taken with the design and embellishment of these pieces, and elaborate inscriptions and pertinent sayings were an integral part of a decorative theme that often included the recipient's name and occasionally that of the potter.

With a masterful sense of design, the potter organized an elaborate ornamental vocabulary that included such flowers and fruits as the familiar pomegranate, tulip, fuchsia, olive leaf, forget-me-not, and lily of the valley. Decorative patterns relied heavily on favorite animals and birds—dove, deer, rabbit, fish, eagle, rooster—and the horse and rider. Appropriate inscriptions of humorous homespun philosophy were introduced by the creative potter as a foil for his decorative treatment.

The potter used two essentially related techniques to apply his patterns to the flat or rounded surface of his wares; slip decoration and sgraffito. Both methods have been known since ancient times, and descended into the hands of the Pennsylvania Germans by way of central European ceramic artisans. Slip decoration was applied by means of one or several goose quills that fed a thin clay fluid from a slip cup. The potter manipulated this cup deftly until the fluid flowed in scrolls, squiggles, or dots to delineate his design. The thin white or creamy solution was a special type of clay, or "slip," imported from New Jersey. As the potter worked his slip cup, his deft movements produced a calligraphic language, not unlike writing done with a broad-pointed nib. He was also able to make thin hairlines with which he would outline figures and decorations. Great skill was required in this operation, as the craftsman's strokes, once applied to the surface, were permanent. When fired, the slip became a light cream or buff color, which contrasted with the darker background of the base.

The second method of decorating pottery surfaces is sgraffito, a term derived from the Italian *sgraffiare*, "to scratch." This technique was used extensively by the Pennsylvania German potters and involves incising a design into a semiwet clay surface by means of a thin sharp-edged wooden tool. First a cream or golden-yellow slip color was applied, then the hairline design was scratched through it, exposing the rust color of the redware; then the piece was fired. The potter worked to achieve a simplicity and clarity of expression —every line, floral form, bird, or figure was rendered with a minimum of strokes.

An entirely new pottery form was created in the process of filling requests for gift ceramics: the circular dish or pie plate. Because of the many variations of the popular tulip motif that decorated this kind of plate, it came to be called tulipware. Created as display pieces, tulipware offered an excellent opportunity for the ceramic craftsman to exhibit his talents. Peacocks, eagles, roosters, and leaf and floral designs in infinitive variety were rendered with a freshness and unmistakable naiveté that came to be characteristic of the work of the Pennsylvania region. Another distinctive feature of these concave dishes was the use of concentric outer rings. They invited the use of pertinent sayings that added an extra fillip to the decorative scheme. Johannes Neesz inscribed one thus: "Luck and misfortune is

every morning our breakfast." As a border for a bird and tulip design John Leidy wrote: "Every bird knows to rest for a short hour after eating." The same potter inscribed this sentiment about independence: "Rather would I single live than my wife the breeches give." Another bit of sly humor accompanies a courtship scene: "God hath created all the beautiful maidens. They are for the potter, but not for the priests." The drinking mug, often elaborately decorated, presented a more difficult problem for inscriptions. One noted piece reads: "I say what is true, and drink what is clear." These expressions were penned in the Pennsylvania German dialect.

Quite by accident, about the turn of this century, this dialect led to the first scholarly interest in these charming pieces. Dr. Edwin Barber, then curator of the Pennsylvania Museum, discovered one of these curious plates in a junk shop. He assumed the piece to be of European origin, but, on deciphering the inscription, realized that instead of High German, this was indeed one of the local dialects, and that the object had been made in a nearby pottery at least a hundred years before. A search was undertaken to locate additional ware to form the basis for a museum collection. After scouring the countryside, Barber was able, from conversations with descendants of potters and their families, to reach a new appraisal of his discovery. Barber also found that the folk traditions displayed in the pottery handicrafts of the Pennsylvania German settlers were the result of a strong cultural heritage that resisted the whims of fashion and preserved those values that suited the settlers' temperaments.

2446 *Tulips, in both natural and conventionalized forms, figured conspicuously as the most prominent decorative motif on Pennsylvania earthenware* 2447 *Feathery leaf and floral forms are an inspired improvisation of the potter with a flair for decoration* 2448–2453 *Fanciful bird forms often are a central feature of these ceramic plates, surrounded with circular borders of flowers, mottoes, or geometric elements. A wide variety of aviary favorites are shown, including the eagle,* 2451 *(c. 1830), the dove,* 2448 *(1813), the peacock,* 2452 *(1812), the parrot,* 2453 *(1808), and the imaginary double bird,* 2449. *"Deer's Chase,"* 2450 *(c. 1800), was the work of David Spinner*

2450

2451

2452

2453

2454 2455

2456

2457

2458

2459 2460

2454–2467 *Many of the pie plates of Pennsylvania potters are recognizable by design, composition, lettering, or other characteristics. David Spinner of Bucks County,* **2454** *(c. 1810), drew figures of soldiers, cavaliers, fashionable women, and picturesque hunting scenes. John Leidy,* **2462** *(1786), was an outstanding craftsman who decorated in sgraffito and the more difficult technique of slip painting. Johannes Neesz,*

2463, 2465, *may have been associated with David Spinner, as his work bears a close resemblance. Georg Hübener,* **2461** *(1786), was a master decorator and skilled at lettering; his handsome inscriptions often carry a comic valentine message. Samuel Troxel,* **2457** *(1826),* **2459** *(1828), had a fondness for birds, specifically the American eagle; he always dated his pieces, often to the very day*

2468   2469

2470   2471

2468–2475 *Slip-decorated ware was made by trickling liquid clay, called slip, through a quill attached to a cup, and required a sure sense of design and direction. True slip is usually distinguished by light-colored ornamentation upon a darker ground, the resultant design taking on a light relief. In contrast, sgraffito ware is the result of incising lines into the soft clay surface before firing. The lines thus depressed, or intaglioed, show dark against a white or yellowish field. Slipware plates are* **2468, 2469, 2472, 2473;** *sgraffito-ware pieces are* **2470, 2471, 2474, 2475**

2472

2473

2474   2475

Overleaf: GALLERY OF CERAMIC PLATES AND DISHES. *Animal motifs:* **2492, 2502, 2504, 2522, 2526;** *birds:* **2481, 2483, 2484, 2500, 2514, 2515, 2518;** *decorative and floral:* **2476, 2478, 2480, 2482, 2485–2491, 2493–2499, 2501, 2503, 2505–2512, 2516, 2517, 2519, 2523, 2525;** *figures:* **2479, 2524;** *linear:* **2477, 2513, 2520, 2521**

2476

2477

2478

2479

2480

2484

2485

2486

2487

2488

2494

2495

2496

2497

2504

2505

2506

2507

2513

2514

2515

2516

2517

2481

2482

2483

2493

2489

2490

2491

2492

2503

2499

2500

2501

2502

2509

2510

2511

2512

2519

2520

2521

2522

2523

2524

2525

2526

679

2527

2528

2527 *Polychromed rooster carved in the well-established tradition of the Pennsylvania German wood-carvers. Every detail in this exquisite piece suggests the hand of a master. The haughty position of the head, sinuous curves of the neck and breast, the peacock-like spread of the splendid tail feathers, the delicate patterning of surfaces, all combine to create an outstanding expression of the whittler's art of the nineteenth century. Photograph courtesy the Abby Aldrich Rockefeller Folk Art Collection, Williamsburg, Virginia*

2529

Whittled for Pastime & Profit

2530

WHITTLING HAS BEEN described variously as a pastime for boys, as everyman's natural instinct, or as a sophisticated way of producing wood shavings. With a sharp knife, anyone can use his leisure time to fashion miniature objects such as mantel decorations, kitchen accessories, toys, and fanciful pieces that have no practical purpose.

The output of the amateur Pennsylvania Dutch whittlers was tremendous, although only a few were above the ordinary. Among these were Wilhelm Schimmel, Aaron Mountz, Noah Weis, and George Huguenin, all of whom were active during the latter part of the nineteenth century. Whether their professional competence is related to their Alpine and Bavarian backgrounds, or whether it indicates a skill developed by experience and observation, the results are worthy of serious study.

The names of most whittlers are unknown, but in some instances their identity has been preserved either by an occasional marking or a recognizable technique. A general design characteristic or possibly the incisional manner of chip carving may also provide a clue to the whittler's identity.

2528 *Eagle carved by Wilhelm Schimmel follows a very personal formula—a crisscross decorative pattern simulates body feathers, while the wing-feather structure consists of rugged prismatic forms serrated at the ends* **2529** *Eagle and squirrel on nest of leaves, surrounded with buds; another subject of which Schimmel carved a small number* **2530** *Eagle carved from single block of pine by Aaron Mountz, latter part of the nineteenth century*

The work of these folk craftsmen falls into several categories according to the treatment of the wood: carved, whittled, scratch-carved, or turned. One of the most skilled carvers was Wilhelm Schimmel. He used a naive cross-hatched patterning scheme when simulating feathers on a bird or the shaggy mane on a horse or dog, creating a surface more characteristic of the peasant approach to stylization than an accurate representation.

Aaron Mountz was a friend and disciple of Schimmel's, and began whittling with his encouragement. Both carved the same general type of subject, such as birds, barnyard animals, squirrels, dogs, and sheep. Whereas Schimmel often affected a rough manner, Mountz's style was painstaking and precise.

Another noted carver was George Huguenin, a descendant of a French-Swiss family, who arrived in this country about the middle of the nineteenth century. He brought with him the wood-carving skill of his native Switzerland, its technique and traditions, customs and subject matter. Most of his time was devoted to making figures for miniature crèches that were usually placed at the base of the Christmas tree. Huguenin's toys were in the European tradition. His barnyard creatures were realistic, particularly his sheep, on which he glued woolly coats. Often he made a barn to hold the flock as well as other toys.

More utilitarian but no less decorative are the surface carvings in wood made for kitchen articles. Wooden cake and cookie molds and marzipan boards were used as matrices for *Lebkuchen* and gingerbread cookies. The springerle boards were subdivided into from six to twenty-four squares, and each one had a different design. The motifs for the boards may have been inspired by nursery fables, animals and birds, or even by Biblical scenes in the more elaborate pieces. The finest examples of these springerle boards were the work of professional carvers and can be found in today's antique markets.

In addition to flat cookie boards, designs were carved on cylindrical rollers which were fitted with handles and looked like rolling pins. Another type of surface decoration related to the cake and cookie boards is found on

butter molds. These might be the property of a single household for its own table use or might be found on print butter that was sold at the local market. The mold designs often became a trademark by which the buyer could distinguish one brand from another. Molds were carved in varying forms, from rectangular to circular. The butter was packed into the circular form with a paddle, and then ejected by a simple plunger which left its imprint. The design, carved in intaglio, appeared in relief on the butter. Designs varied greatly. One of the most interesting motifs is the star-shaped symbol of the sun, which was used to protect the butter from spoilage.

Wood carving also appeared on sugar mortars, dippers, bowls, ladles, and paddles. In addition to carved kitchen utensils, there were clock frames, spoon racks, mirror frames, weathercocks, gateposts, and a myriad of other objects which appealed to the craftsman.

It is worth noting the marked contrast between the peasant carving of the Pennsylvania farmland areas and those of the New England region. In the former group, we find the minor decorative arts: toys, mantel ornaments, cake and butter molds, and a Noah's Ark filled with animals and birds. Occasionally a sculptured figure appears in the round, like that of Blind Justice, a rare example of pure three-dimensional carving, attributed to John Fisher of York, Pennsylvania. No architectural carving existed because the farm dwellings, mostly of native stone, did not permit exterior ornamentation; the hex signs on barn exteriors were the only notes of decoration to be found. On the New England seaboard, however, cities enjoyed a flourishing trade with Europe and naturally developed a broader cultural base. Garden statuary, decorations designed for architectural placement, figureheads and marine decoration in all its many phases, trade signs, and all manner of lesser types of carved work were found throughout the area. Trade and other dealings with foreign sources encouraged an exchange of ideas and skills, whereas the farmland regions maintained their insularity and, with it, a limited horizon in arts and crafts. Both regions, however, have contributed significantly to the mainstream of decorative art in America.

2531

2532

2533

2534

2535

2536

2537

2538

2539

2540

2541

2542

2531-2543 *Domestic birds, especially the barnyard variety, were among the favorite subjects of the traveling whittlers of the Pennsylvania countryside. Hens and roosters, robins and parrots, were second in popularity only to the favored eagle. The many renditions of the rooster were more realistic than those of the eagle, possibly because the latter was rarely available for close study, and so became more idealized. If some birds are difficult to identify, it is because of a design formula the carver adopted*

2543

685

2544

2544–2549 *Aaron Mountz, a disciple of Schimmel and undoubtedly influenced by him, nevertheless developed his own individual style. He was more painstaking and precise. While many of Schimmel's birds defy recognition, a work by Mountz is clearly distinguished by its naturalistic approach. Yet his manner is stylized too, dominated by a strong sense of patterning in the feather treatment. His subjects included eagles, parrots, owls, herons or cranes, and poodles—and even the last carried the crosshatching of fur and mane*

2545

2546

2547

2548

2549

2550

2551

2552

Wandering Wood-carver

Those carvers who traveled extensively in order to peddle their wares seem to have attained greater competence than those who did not. For one German settler in the Pennsylvania region, Wilhelm Schimmel, carving odd bits became a way of life. Little is known of Schimmel's background, but he may have come from the Black Forest or Bavarian section of southern Germany, where wood carving had been practiced for centuries. Schimmel came to live in the Cumberland valley, near Carlisle, shortly after the Civil War, and from then until his death in 1890 he shuttled over the countryside, going from house to house peddling his talent with a jackknife. Sometimes he carried little birds and animals ready-made for quick sale. At other times he would ask for any large piece of pine lying about, offering to transform it into

2553

2550, 2551 *The rugged rough-hewn character of Schimmel's eagles is a reflection of the man himself, who was noted for his temper as well as for his excellent handicraft. Figure 2550 from a photograph, courtesy the Smithsonian Institution, Washington, D.C.* **2551** *Eagle carved by Schimmel carries the unmistakable characteristics of outstretched wings, serrated feather ends, small body, and large head with a tuft* **2552** *Garden of Eden is Schimmel's naive attempt at storytelling, replete with fence, figures, apple, snake, and tree embellished at the top with pine shavings. The carver made several of these* **2553** *There is a strong suggestion of the parrot in this upright eagle, particularly due to treatment of head and beak*

an eagle that might measure as much as three feet across. When he came to town with a basket of birds, he traded his handiwork for meals or just for pennies. Sometimes he would pass a splendid carving across the bar in exchange for a pint of whisky.

Schimmel was said to be surly, blasphemous, and ill tempered. Children learned to avoid him, but a few people understood and befriended him. John Greider, a miller and farmer living just west of Carlisle, opened his doors to the rude itinerant carver. After Schimmel had made one of his tours of the neighboring towns, he would return to the Greider homestead and volunteer to help with the farm chores.

The technical marks of Schimmel's handiwork are obvious and easy to detect. He first shaped the body of a bird, then carved the wings as separate members. These were pegged or doweled into position. When finished with the detailing, Schimmel applied a coat of gesso, a plaster wash he preferred to use before applying the final coat of paint, in order to brighten his birds and beasts. Black, brown, red, and yellow ocher were his favorite colors, though his palette often depended on what the farmer had available, whether barn red or an indiscriminate leftover.

Schimmel's fame rests particularly on his eagles, which are now in leading public and private American collections. He also executed all types of barnyard animals and occasionally wild ones such as lions, wolves, and foxes of indefinable features; toy soldiers were also among his creations. Just before his death he fashioned an Adam and Eve before the tree where they were tempted; the grouping was surrounded by a picket fence with corner posts mounted on a rectangular base. This and other Biblical scenes were popular with the people of the region, but Schimmel's character did not favor lessons from the Bible; he was more at home with the eagles and roosters on which his fame rests.

2554 *The pose of this Schimmel eagle differs from his favorite attitude, shown below. Wide wingspread and low body are unusual, yet all other characteristics of the carver are in evidence, including crosshatched patterning on body, coarse carving on wings and parrot-like beak structure. Photograph*
2555 *Crosshatching on the tail of this squirrel by Schimmel gives more of a pine-cone than a fur effect*
2556 *At least two dozen of this Schimmel eagle are now in the hands of collectors and museums*

2555

2556

2557

2559

2557 *In the eighteenth-century parlor of the Kershner house in Berks County, Pennsylvania, is furniture typical of the period and region. Grouped about the walnut sawbuck table are side chairs described as Moravian and an armchair at the table's end, a country version of the Philadelphia Chippendale form. In the corner stands the traditional German wardrobe usually included in the bride's dowry, and, next to it, the leather-covered armchair that belonged to self-styled "baron" Henry Steigel, the glassware manufacturer. The blanket, or dower, chest is dated 1774, and on its top is a Bible box with a 1748 German Bible. The tall clock, with inlays, is by Jacob Graff, of Lebanon. The table is set with wooden plates, horn cups, pewter tankards, and green glass bottles. Photograph courtesy the Henry Francis du Pont Winterthur Museum, Winterthur, Delaware*

692   2558

2560

Furniture

"Plain & Fancy"

THE VAST WOODLANDS of the Pennsylvania colony, from the fertile rolling countryside bordering on the Delaware westward over the mountainous regions reaching to the Monongahela, were rich in softwoods and hardwoods suitable for fuel, fencing, construction, and furniture. The supply was so abundant as to justify calling the Colonial era in America the "age of wood."

After several generations of working with woods that were new to them, both joiner and cabinetmaker had learned their individual peculiarities, their textures, strength, grain, their staining and polishing characteristics. Cedar resisted moisture and thus was suitable for fence posts, shingles, pails, tubs, and cisterns. Woods like pine and oak had many uses, not only for furniture but as joists, sills, and rafters in the construction of barns and

2558 *Pennsylvania plank chair featuring stylized tulip heart* **2559** *Wall cupboard with central panel carved with birds and gouge marks* **2560** *Spoon rack with decorations of chip-carved Frisian lunettes*

693

buildings. Ash and hickory were ideal for tool handles and where great strength was needed. For the making of furniture, pine and whitewood, that is, tulip poplar or yellow poplar, were most used among the softwoods. Fine cabinetry called for hardwood such as black walnut, cherry, and maple; their bird's-eye and tiger-striped variants were the result of a particular way of cutting and sawing. Mahogany, so extensively used by the Philadelphia cabinet, makers for the formal pieces in the style of Chippendale and Hepplewhite, were not used in the style and period under discussion here.

By the middle of the eighteenth century, many of the agricultural settlements of eastern Pennsylvania were emerging from their primitive conditions. Farmers were now able to order better furnishings for their homes from the local cabinetmaker. Moderately affluent pioneers tried to recapture the amenities of their homelands and to create heirlooms that could be passed down to their children.

Tables and chairs were made first, then a *Schrank* (wardrobe) for storing clothes, as closets were virtually unknown. Cupboards and dressers came next in the succession of things most needed, followed by smaller objects like Bible chests and wall racks for spoons, stools, and occasional pieces. The priorities varied, naturally, according to the Colonist's circumstances, and also depended on the local craftsman and the extent of his commitments. Family custom among the early Pennsylvanians dictated that a daughter should have a dowry at the time of her marriage. The dower chest, of simple dovetail construction and decorated in styles that varied from county to county, headed an inventory of items that

2561 *Poplar wagon seat with splint webbing, splayed, ring-turned legs, and cresting rail with pierced heart, c. 1780*

2561

included a wardrobe, table, bed, and a stated number of quilts and coverlets woven by the bride to be. These essential country furnishings became the nucleus around which the bride's future home was built. Fortunately, because of the great care with which these chests were designed and treasured, they survive as a record of a way of life of two centuries ago, rich in detailed notations and documentation.

A cursory glance at the table setting and furniture of the Kershner parlor, typical of a family in moderate circumstances, shows a marked parallel with room furnishings of contemporary southern Germany. The local craftsman, like his patron living on a farm or in a small village isolated from the outside world, reflected the prevailing Baroque taste. Hardly a trace of contemporary fashion filtered through to him, and thus his design concepts were uncontaminated by the whims of the day, especially the popular acceptance of the masters of English cabinetry. Thus the Germanic prototypes were reproduced as closely as memory allowed in the earlier years of colonization and, as recollection served, well into the nineteenth century.

The plank-seat chairs in the Kershner parlor followed a Moravian type, with sharply splayed legs, heavy flat seat, shaped splat back silhouetted in graceful outline. A reinforced crosspiece under the seat served to anchor the legs. The massive armchair for the head of the table had front legs that were turned in simple fashion and heavy arms that sometimes ended in a knob or scroll. It had a flat back with a shaped splat, a solid seat, and square-shaped shaped splat, a solid seat, and square-shaped rungs. The sawbuck table, which was often very long, had thick crossed legs held rigidly in position by a central stretcher and pegged pins for tightening at both ends. This table type antedated the four-legged tables that were usually equipped with drawers under the plank tops for storing linens and cutlery.

The huge wardrobe, or *Schrank*, was an important piece that took on mammoth proportions. It, too, followed closely along the lines of central European pieces. It rested on corner brackets and had a heavy cornice, large double doors, and several drawers at the bottom. The facing of doors and stiles was hip-paneled or treated with stained or painted moldings. Often the entire surface of the wardrobe was decorated with exquisite traceries of familiar folk motifs, painted with superb skill or inlaid by a rare technique called "wax inlay," in which the wax hardened and mellowed to resemble ivory.

Corner cupboards and open-shelf dressers were built to display choice bits of decorated pottery and pewter. It was customary to notch the edge of one of the open-dresser shelves to form a spoon rack. Hanging wall cupboards, chests of drawers, and smaller items such as Bible boxes, candle boxes, spice holders, pipe racks, and mirrors were usually decorated rather than left as plain wood surfaces.

A favorite among the Pennsylvania cabinetmakers was the straight-grained black walnut. It became very dark when highly polished, however, and this darkness accounted for fluctuations in its popularity. Where black walnut was not available, both yellow and black cherry wood were used. When well aged, black cherry approaches mahogany in color, and its workability is quite similar.

Characteristic of all this region's furniture was its strictly utilitarian quality. Sturdy construction was never sacrificed, even in dower chests that were meant to be embellished. A fondness for color and gaiety in furnishings nevertheless manifested itself, not only in the decorated dower chests, but in cupboards, dressers, and smaller objects that could be treated more intimately. Such furniture may be said to be "paint decorated." It received several coats of a base paint which acted as a preservative, and then the decoration was added, "just for fancy." It is most difficult to draw the line between "plain" and "fancy," but generally the love for conceits and whimsies appears more often in minor objects that lent themselves to ornamentation than in functional pieces of furniture.

2562

2563

2564

2565

2562 *Peasant-type walnut table (c. 1730–40) with shaped square legs supported by heavy stretchers. The apron is richly decorated with curvatures. Wide table-top planks are held together with cleats* **2563** *Oak sawbuck table (c. 1750) with cross side supports of heavy stock held together by center stretcher and pegged darts at ends. Foot rests also serve to give additional support as stretchers* **2564** *Decorated Pennsylvania dresser with glass doors, reeded quarter columns at corners, and hand-painted ornaments, including figures of angels taken from birth certificates, c. 1828* **2565** *Corner cabinet with open shelves at top; door and side panels with painted decorations*

2566

2567

2568

2566 *Oval-top pine table shaped in the traditional provincial form, with splayed legs and bottom stretchers. Apron decorated with typical curves and scrolls of the region. Dated 1750* **2567** *Hanging corner cabinet of pine is graced by an especially delightful display area at top, delicately scrolled and topped by fitting cap molding, c. 1750* **2568** *Open kitchen dresser for the display of plates, kitchenware, and spoons. Decorated cresting under cornice and on side pieces shows heavy plank construction*

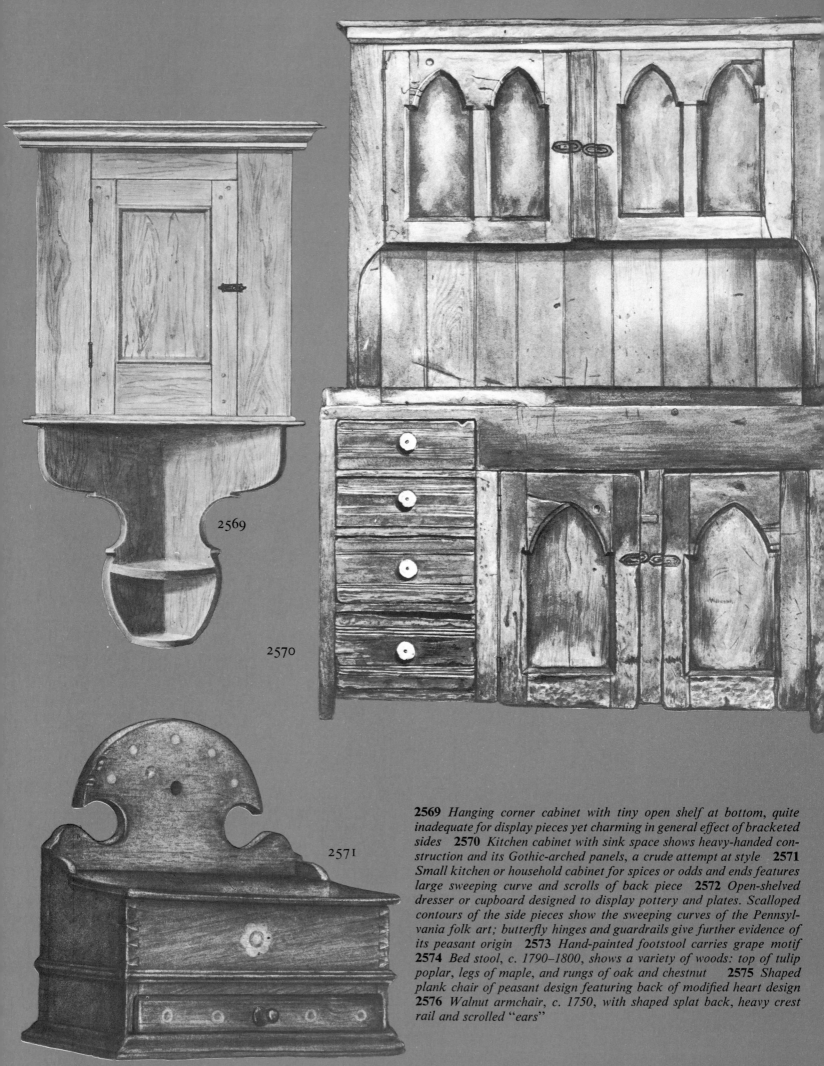

2569 Hanging corner cabinet with tiny open shelf at bottom, quite inadequate for display pieces yet charming in general effect of bracketed sides **2570** Kitchen cabinet with sink space shows heavy-handed construction and its Gothic-arched panels, a crude attempt at style. **2571** Small kitchen or household cabinet for spices or odds and ends features large sweeping curve and scrolls of back piece **2572** Open-shelved dresser or cupboard designed to display pottery and plates. Scalloped contours of the side pieces show the sweeping curves of the Pennsylvania folk art; butterfly hinges and guardrails give further evidence of its peasant origin **2573** Hand-painted footstool carries grape motif **2574** Bed stool, c. 1790–1800, shows a variety of woods: top of tulip poplar, legs of maple, and rungs of oak and chestnut **2575** Shaped plank chair of peasant design featuring back of modified heart design **2576** Walnut armchair, c. 1750, with shaped splat back, heavy crest rail and scrolled "ears"

2572

2573

2574

2575

2576

2577

2578

2577 *The traditional Pennsylvania German style of decoration is much in evidence in this Fraktur room, so called because of the many baptismal certificates, house blessings, and framed sentiments written in Fraktur calligraphy. Typical also in this Berks County room are the two hand-painted dower chests at the rear. Second half of the eighteenth century. Photograph courtesy the Henry Francis du Pont Winterthur Museum, Winterthur, Delaware* **2578** *Of the same period is this painted splint box, showing a man in a red coat with cane and tricorn hat and suggesting the festive occasion when this type of box was given* **2579** *In many dower chests the architectonic division of space into panels effectively separated decorative elements. This one, made in 1787*

Decorated for Dowry

2579

THE DOWER CHEST was a traditional part of every maiden's world; she began to fill it with linens and laces the moment she learned to sew. When she stitched her first sampler or embroidered her first linens, these were carefully stored in the chest until she was married. Dower chests were the first hope chests designed to serve both a utilitarian and a romantic function and great care went into their construction and decoration. They were generally three to four feet long and were placed in either the parlor or the bedroom. Some chests contained a built-in drawer or two, but this was not typical. To raise the chest off the floor and give it a more convenient height, various supports were used—the shoe or trestle foot, the ball foot, the ogee bracket, or ordinary bracket foot could be placed at the four bottom corners. All of these could easily be constructed from flat stock with a scroll or fret saw.

The woods most used for dower chests were pine, poplar, and walnut. The large expanse of the front and top surface of each chest invited the hand of the decorator, and at the same time a painted surface made the soft wood more durable. The farmer-carpenter, however, rarely

attempted to decorate the chest himself, but preferred to wait for the itinerant decorator to make his accustomed rounds.

The painted chest of the Pennsylvania Germans varied little from eighteenth-century European peasant furniture which was made of inexpensive pine and decorated in color. The favorite background color was a soft blue; dark green, brown, and even black were used on occasion. On this background, the decorator deftly applied vases of flowers, stars, tulips, daisies, birds, angels, and unicorns. The front panel was often divided into an architectonic arrangement of two or three arched areas. The end panels utilized the same architectonic forms to extend the impact of the front facade. Often the decorator designed an interplay of motifs which extended from the front areas to the end panels.

In Pennsylvania, the tulip recalled the distant gardens of the Rhineland and was used extensively. The fuchsia and carnation were also popular. The heart, symbol of love, appeared in every medium employed by the folk artist. The huge star featured on the com-

modious barns in Lehigh and Montgomery counties appeared as a favorite motif in chest decoration. The unicorns on Berks County chests are a carry-over from medieval days, when they represented the guardians of maidenhood. The peacock, stitched on hand towels and painted on chests and toleware, was a respected weather prophet.

Most chests were painted to order; often the owner's name appeared with the date and year of execution. The lettering on many of these chests was often in the Germanic or *Fraktur* style, using Gothic letter forms. Christian Selzer (1749–1831) inscribed and painted some of the finest dower chests in the Pennsylvania region.

Another fine decorator was Heinrich Otto, who also had a printing shop in Ephrata. His favorite design motifs were parrots, peacocks, animated birds with twisted necks, floral forms, and leafy vines.

Except for a few names, the painter-decorators whose works are now on display in museum collections or in private homes remain anonymous.

2580

2581

2582

2580–2585 *All marriage chests had lift lids; some featured bottom drawers, but otherwise their construction varied little. There is great ingenuity in their scheme of decoration, however, and diverse motifs are used. Double-arched panels, as in* **2581, 2584,** *and* **2585,** *and triple arches, as in* **2582** *and* **2583,** *assist in well-ordered design schemes in which urns, flowered arrangements, and unicorns appear.*

704

2583

2584

2585

2586

2587

2586–2591 *In the dower chest for Ann Beer (1790), the decorator floats a pair of mermaids holding sprays of flowers. Geometric elements characterize* **2589**; *plants and floral forms dominate in* **2587**, **2588**, **2590**, *and* **2591** *with unicorns, hearts, and tulips interspersed. Most of these chests were made and decorated before 1800*

2588

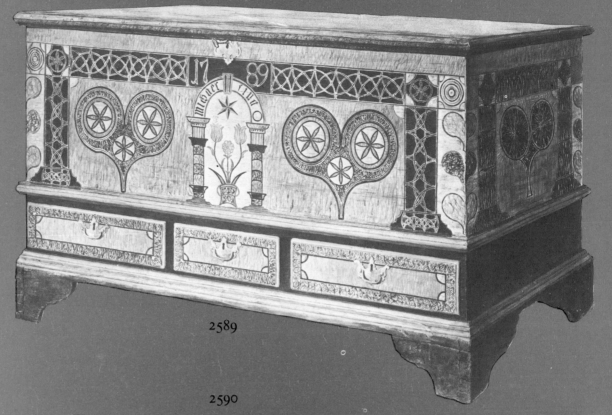

2589

2590

2591

707

2592

2593

2592–2597 *The floral sprigs and plant forms of Pennsylvania dower chests exhibit an informal boldness and sprightliness. Feathery leaves and twisting stems are the rule, and where the ornament is confined to a panel, it generally grows from an urn or vase and takes a symmetrical shape. The human figure is rare, but can be seen in* **2594** *and as a rider in* **2595.** *Unicorn chests (see* **2596***), named after their dominant motif, are often intricately ornamented*

2594

2595

2596

2597

2598

2599

2598–2603 *A group of chests made and decorated between 1775 and 1787 follows no rigid scheme. Swirling petaled blossoms in* **2600** *almost suggest a child's pinwheel. The all-over repetition of small units,* **2598,** *is quite unique; the introduction of shells and insects,* **2602,** *is unusual in this region. In* **2599** *and especially in* **2603,** *the exceptionally elaborate use of flowers and birds creates panels with a quality of fine tapestry. Wherever escutcheon plates are used, they are often available furniture forms and thus not compatible with the peasant character of the chest*

2600

2601

2602

2603

711

2604

2605

2606

2607

For Bibles,

Books &

Bibelots

712

2608

2609

2604–2610 *The small box or chest came in many forms and has variously been called a desk box, Bible box, gift box, and treasure chest. Lids were either hinged or sliding tops. Floral decoration was lavish. The ubiquitous tulip form was employed, and occasionally geometric devices, as in* **2607** *and* **2608***. The candle box,* **2606***, combines the best of many favorite motifs. The casket with domed lid,* **2608***, is covered with wallpaper. A salt box for the kitchen is shown in* **2609**

2610

2611

2612

2613

714

2614

2611–2616 *The four sides and top of the carved trinket chest, **2611**, are embellished with birds and floral sprigs. Painted candle boxes, **2613** and **2616**, were also used to hold jewels. End panel, **2612**, is decorated with flowers, buds, and leafy vines. The dough trough of poplar, **2614,** was decorated by Christian Selzer. The decorator of the domed casket, **2615,** has departed from traditional motifs in favor of abstract devices of rings and cusps, vigorously painted*

2615

2616

2617

2618

716

Scribe & Scroll

THE PENNSYLVANIA DUTCH followed the ancient practice of recording vital statistics in family registers, using excellent handmade paper and illuminated inks, tints, and dyes so that the records would survive. This tradition encouraged the creation of lively, original genealogies in forms that are authentic and artistic.

Much credit must be given to the Pennsylvania papermakers, for without their skill, these beautiful writings and records would have been lost. Among a group of Mennonite colonists that settled there was William Ritten-

house, who was descended from a long line of German papermakers. With the help of German workmen, Rittenhouse set up a mill on the banks of the Schuylkill River. Paper was in demand in all the Colonies, especially because of the uncertainty of shipments from overseas, and local printing houses needed it for printing currency and for their other work.

The highest grade of paper was made from linen and cotton rags and remnants, by a slow process of disintegration, fermentation, and the beating down of the textile fibers. The rags were macerated between two millstones and immersed in troughs of water. After being

2617, 2618 *Birth and baptismal certificates, called* Taufschein, *are intricately lettered and embellished in the traditional* Fraktur *style* **2619–2621** *Details from* Fraktur *paintings show a love of floral and naturalistic ornament*

2620   2621

thoroughly cleansed, the whole was beaten into pulp by large wooden hammers until a homogeneous mass resulted. The mass was then put into a wooden frame with a base of woven wire netting that permitted only water to drip through. The skilled papermaker then manipulated the frame so that the fibrous particles of pulp were evenly deposited and became a thin layer on the frame. The basic sheet of wet paper was then removed by a woolen web, or felt, and dried.

The beautiful records of the Pennsylvania Dutch are done in *Fraktur*. *Fraktur-schrift*, as it was called in Germany, was a form of creative calligraphy named after the sixteenth-century *Fraktur* typeface. The latter was a crude imitation of the current manuscript writing styles, more cursive than the stiff Gothic black letter, and was cut in metal by the German type founders shortly after Gutenberg's time. When the Germans settled in southeastern Pennsylvania, the writing of family records, *Taufschein,* or birth and baptismal certificates, *Bücherzeichen*, or bookplates, house blessings, and valentines continued. Highly ornamental, hand drawn and colored, these calligraphic pieces were executed by the educated members of the community, the schoolmaster and the clergyman, or by itinerant artists.

The schoolmaster was expected to be versatile. He prepared legal papers, wrote letters for people who could not write, and executed the hand-written documents, especially those pertaining to births and baptisms, that were in constant demand.

To teach writing and the styles of the alphabet and at the same time to demonstrate his skill as a penman and decorator, the schoolmaster prepared a *Vorschrift*, or handwritten model, that was the forerunner of the nineteenth-century copybook. From the *Vorschriften*, pupils learned how to form numerals and letters of the alphabet in German script and *Fraktur* writing. An ever-present feature was

the large ornamental German capital, heading a well-lettered pious German text. The schoolmaster frequently signed his name to the *Vorschrift* to testify to his fluent craftsmanship. The *Vorschrift* was often presented to a pupil as a reward and token of the instructor's regard. It was framed with other examples of the calligrapher's art, and hung on the family walls. The *Haus-Segen* (house blessings) were treasured wallpieces, for devout Germans felt more secure when they could follow these religious invocations daily.

Each *Fraktur* practitioner seems to have adhered closely to his own style of drawing and decoration, and this repertoire of motifs became identifiable over a period of time. As long as his decorative idiom was acceptable, the practical workman saw no reason to introduce new elements, and he would expect a promising pupil to copy them too. But because the copyist's imitation was never exact, and because, as he became more proficient, he made changes of his own, there was always an infusion of fresh ideas.

Painting and drawing at Sunday afternoon sessions were permitted, although all other forms of amusement and entertainment were strictly forbidden. Invariably the finely executed religious precepts in *Fraktur* were set before the young scriveners to copy. A kind-hearted schoolmaster would often present a drawing of a bird or flower as a prize for diligence and good conduct. These little tokens were carefully preserved from generation to generation.

The Pennsylvania German style decorations on the *Fraktur* manuscripts cover a wide range of subject matter. The renditions, however, take on distinct technomorphic variations because the sharp-pointed pen made linear characteristics quite different from those translated by the brush or the sgraffito incisions on ceramics. Greater detail, more minute and microscopic handling of leaf and floral forms, accompany the letter forms on *Vorschriften*,

Taufschein, *Haus-Segen*, and *Bücherzeichen*. Floral motifs were generally conventionalized, except for the tulip; its shape was close enough to botanical form to be recognizable.

The *Fraktur* artist's inspiration came from many sources, including textile pattern books published in Switzerland, Germany, France, and England in the period from 1580 to 1750. Highly stylized decorative birds—parrots, peacocks, doves, hens and chickens, and eagles—and particularly the *Distelfink* (goldfinch), were favorite motifs. Animals included lambs, lions, and deer. The unicorn and other motifs were borrowed from heraldic sources. Strangely enough, these aristocratic symbols represented the very classes from whom the freedom-loving Germans had escaped. On occasion, other motifs appeared, such as stags, mermaids, and angels, though the human figure was rare because a higher degree of skill was required for its delineation.

Like many other Colonial craftsmen, the scriveners were often itinerants who made a meager living traveling about peddling their handiwork. Often they prepared their documents before setting out, leaving blank spaces to be filled in according to the purchaser's needs. Ornamental examples of their work, like quotations from the Bible, blessings, and hymnals, were framed, and often the only pictorial objects on farmhouse walls. Of the itinerants, a latecomer to the fertile Pennsylvania countryside was August Bauman, a Hungarian by birth who adapted to the German customs. Late in the nineteenth century, he traveled by horse and buggy from village to village, plying his craft and catering to a fast-disappearing demand. This outmoded profession was his sole source of livelihood, and the fact that he was able to pick up commissions indicates the strength of the tradition.

There are a number of outstanding names associated with *Fraktur* arts and crafts. One of the best known is that of Francis Portzline, who was born in Düsseldorf, Germany, in 1771, and lived to be ninety-six. Hundreds of birth and baptismal certificates were made by Portzline; many of them are signed, but even those that are not are unmistakably his. The basic large heart-shaped cartouche, or enclosure, was designed to bear the text, with an interlaced Celtic knot at its lower tip. Surrounding the heart was an assortment of floral and animal motifs that were fairly consistent throughout his long career: tulip sprays, parrots, naturalistic birds, conventionalized hex symbols, and a sprinkling of smaller elements. All were rendered with a sure line and with bold drawing and coloring; the spatial relationships were almost as well studied in later life as in his prime. A noted example shows the *Hausfrau* at the bottom of a certificate, in well-tailored costume and apron, holding a floral wreath on which is perched a bird.

Heinrich Otto, of Lancaster County, was a contemporary of Portzline, a decorator whose broad interests included not only *Fraktur* work but the painting and decorating of chests and other furniture. He extended his medium by designing and cutting woodblocks with *Fraktur* motifs, and then printing *Fraktur*-type broadsides which he colored by hand. Printed specimens dated as early as 1784 show a prolific sense of design; movable floral and animal blocks are incorporated and juggled in a variety of arrangements that are rarely repeated. The cherub's head, parrots and peacocks, flowers and wreaths, provide restless, expressive language.

Unfortunately, Otto's ingenuity in devising printed shortcuts for the hand-drawn illumination eventually led to the demise of *Fraktur* writing. By the end of the nineteenth century, very few calligraphers were still practicing their art because the printing press had become an increasingly strong competitor. On the wall of the Bucks County Historical Society hangs a touching memorial to the art of *Fraktur*—it shows a paintbox belonging to one of the early illuminators of the county.

2622

2623

2624

2625

2626

720

2628

2627

2629

2630

2622–2630 Fraktur *is distinguished by an elaborate system of embellishment in which intricate calligraphic arrangements are incorporated with floral and animal decoration. The heart was used wherever panels were called for, often as a dominant cartouche around the message, baptismal record, or blessing*

2631

2632

2633

2634

2631 *Elizabetha Schlosser's birth certificate is set in a beautiful composition of hearts and flowers, recorded in 1808* **2632** *Manuscript and miniature illustrating selection from a hymnal, dated 1797* **2633** *Drawing of peacocks and parrots found pasted inside a chest of similar design, 1782* **2634** *Birth and baptismal record executed by Martin Brechall, an excellent penman and teacher, 1806* **2635** *Birth certificate, dated 1766, which*

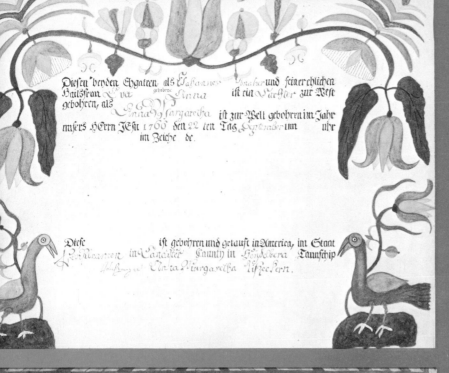

2635

2636

2637

2638

freely uses naturalistic forms and peacocks
2636 *Drawn and colored on wrapping paper, this birth certificate of Lea Herold is an original composition of floral and plant forms* **2637** *Handsome composition of birds, tulips, hearts, and urns with no inscription, may have been merely an exercise of the decorator's skill* **2638** *Tulips, plant forms, and birds decorate this birth and baptismal record, dated 1827*

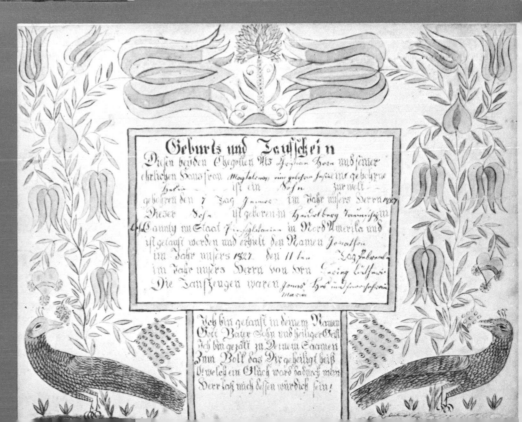

Forgings & Fireplaces

2640

AMONG THE EARLIEST SETTLERS in the Pennsylvania territory were much-needed artisans, including an appreciable number of ironmasters and blacksmiths. They readily found employment and opportunities for setting up their own iron plantations. The region was rich in limestone for flux and timber for making charcoal, and the iron ore often lay just beneath the rusty soil. Little digging was needed to reach the ore, and only a few tools besides a pickax and a crowbar.

Setting up an iron plantation required a location in the midst of several thousand acres of timber, which was then felled to keep the furnaces going. At the time of the Revolution,

there were already eighty-one ironworks operating in Pennsylvania, including blast furnaces, forges, rolling mills, plating mills, steel furnaces, and bloomeries. This is remarkable in view of the British Parliament's Iron Act of 1750, which attempted to prohibit such ironworks in the Colonies so that this valuable trade would remain in British hands. The law was openly flouted, and during the Revolution the well-established foundries were able to supply cannon, mortars, shells, and shot to the American army.

Iron plantations were planned as great self-supporting woodland estates that sustained all the workers in the community. Skilled laborers included woodcutters, teamsters,

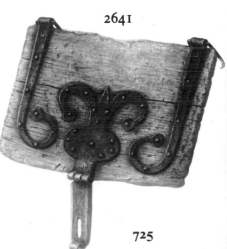

2641

2639 Pat Lyon at the Forge *was painted in 1826 by John Neagle of Philadelphia. It shows the blacksmith in his shop. A glimpse of the jail where Lyon was falsely imprisoned can be seen through the open window. After his release he used the money paid him as restitution to commission this painting by the artist. Museum of Fine Arts, Boston* **2640, 2641** *Decorative wroughtiron hardware and hasps adorned the box lids on Conestoga wagons in eighteenth-century Pennsylvania*

2642

2644

2642 *Cast-iron stoveplate, dated 1751, cast by John Potts, Pottsgrove Furnace. The Biblical reference indicated is "Judge Not." Photograph* 2643 *Stoveplate cast by George Stevenson, 1763, at the Mary Ann Furnace, York County. Photograph*

2643

charcoal burners, colliers, smiths, and ironworkers of all types. The women did the weaving and spinning, the haying and harvesting, and the planting and tilling of the soil, in addition to their housekeeping chores.

In this community the patriarchal blacksmith was a man of substance, skilled in his craft, respected and in great demand. The smith forged axes and tools for clearing the forest, nails and hardware for homes, metal implements for working the soil, iron rims for wagon wheels, and axles for all manner of vehicle. Decorative hasps and hinges were used on Conestoga wagon toolboxes, waffle irons, and fireside equipment such as spits, trammels, brackets, cranes, and pothooks.

The farmer and ironmaster were closely allied because of the constant need for fuel. The smaller furnace owners bought their wood from farmers, who cut it from their timberland. When a farmer had accumulated sufficient capital, he might venture into the lucrative iron industry, providing his land contained enough ore deposits.

As the needs of the settlers grew, some degree of specialization developed among the several hundred smiths. Most were busily engaged in making essential tools and in supplying household needs. The fashioning of bits of hardware and kitchen utensils encouraged some latitude in shapes and forms. Those smiths with a flair for improvisation created functional ironwork with a touch of grace and ornament. Their products show an originality in the adaptations of favorite

2645

2646

2647

regional motifs such as the tulip and heart, and other indigenous forms.

Molten iron does not permit fumbling or hesitation, and the smith had to be a man of decision. He could not work from paper designs but had to carry in his mind a clear picture not only of the final form but the steps necessary in arriving at this design. The tools he needed—hammer and punches, tongs, and chisels—were carefully racked in order, conveniently within his grasp as he worked at the anvil. An apprentice operated the giant bellows which furnished the draft for the fire as the smith forged his piece of iron, gracefully turning and twisting it on his anvil until a latch or delicate fork took shape.

The "village blacksmith" managed somehow to survive until the twentieth century, but today he is a rarity. To recapture the picture of this vanished American, restoration villages have introduced the blacksmith shop as a curiosity along with the country store and the one-room schoolhouse.

While the blacksmith produced individual pieces, the iron-caster's products resulted from pouring molten metal into sand molds, and

2648

2649

thus many casts were created by repeating this operation. A patternmaker was responsible for design of the cast-iron pieces. The patterns were made from wood, lead, or pewter, but the majority were of wood since this could readily be cut, carved, or chiseled to provide the details of decoration and lettering which often accompanied a design. Most patternmakers had a feeling for ornaments and figures and had mastered the Roman alphabet, for inscriptions and quotations were an integral part of Pennsylvanian stoveplates and firebacks. Fine sand provided the material into which the pattern was imbedded, thus forming a matrix into which the hot metal flowed. For the casting of pots and other kitchen utensils, the sand-flask method was used in conjunction with clay molds.

Among the better-known ironmasters were the celebrated Henry W. Stiegel, the self-styled "baron" who operated the Elizabeth Furnace; Thomas Rutter, who started Colebrookdale Furnace in 1720, the earliest in this territory; Thomas Maybury, who operated the Hereford Furnace; and the various members of the Ege family, who owned works in the Cumberland valley: the Mount Holly Iron Works, Carlisle Furnace, Charming Forge, and Pine Grove Furnace.

2648 *The fireback pictures "The Highlander" and was cast at New York in 1767, although there are no records to prove a foundry existed on the island of Manhattan at that time. The plate is adorned with a rich Flemish border surmounted by dolphins. Photograph*

2649 *Cast at the Mary Ann Furnace in York County, 1763. The doubled, arched design, supported by twisted columns and enclosing a floral pattern, is a peculiar convention followed by most Pennsylvania furnaces after they abandoned Biblical scenes in about 1750. The origin of this decoration is unknown, but with minor variations it persisted, as if a trademark, among most furnaces in the region*

Firebacks and stoveplates were produced in great quantities throughout the eighteenth century. The former, usually decorative, were designed to reflect heat from the fireplace into the room. Their efficiency was so questionable that Benjamin Franklin was prompted to design the Franklin stove.

Invented in 1742, the Franklin stove was, in effect, a portable lightweight cast-iron fireplace with back and sides and an extended floor. It could be readily placed into any existing fireplace with piping to connect it to the nearest flue. Thus Franklin's stove provided all the joys of an open fire in addition to the comfort of greater heat; and it used less fuel. On many of the stoves that were produced, the large front face above the opening enabled the patternmaker to do his best ornamental handiwork. Perhaps the best-known decorative styles were those that incorporated the inscriptions "Alter Idem" and "Be Liberty Thine."

The true fireback, commonly used in the area, was positioned at the rear of the fireplace wall, usually higher than wide, with a raised crest or curvature at the top. Its overall shape is similar to that of many gravestones. These were cast for the German immigrants by English and Welsh foundries. The iconography of the German fireplates incorporates a language of devices and floral patterns: tulips, lilies, stars, lozenges, hearts, wheat sheaves, and sunbursts combined with artful imagination. Their designer or designers, the most original of the stoveplate carvers, produced a series of plates that were highly stylized; they were derived from established motifs yet were uniquely different from the European versions. The Renaissance framing, the use of arches, columns, decorative spandrels, the form of the date cartouche, the style of lettering and

2650

2651

2650 *Almost a companion piece to "The Highlander," in 2648, the figure of a maiden is accompanied by the word* Frühling, *meaning* Spring. Photograph **2651** *Stove plate made by Stiegel at the Elizabeth Furnace in 1769 bears a portrait in relief of Stiegel, "The Hero"*

2652

2653   2654

numerals, and the use of banded inscriptions point to earlier plates that were cast both in Germany and in other parts of this country.

The firebacks were cast in single pieces, but the elaborate construction of cast-iron stoves afforded an opportunity for the designer to display his virtuosity. Most popular, at first, was the five-plate stove, a device set into a wall of the fireplace which extended into the adjoining room behind. It had no fuel door or smoke pipe and was fed through the wall from the front. This stove is representative of the first of American-made iron stoves. Jamb stoves, as they were also called, were common in Germany, and many sets of plates were brought to Pennsylvania, where they served as patterns. Biblical subjects with German titles dominated the decorative themes. These stoves were manufactured in the eastern and central part of the colony from 1741 to 1768.

The Biblical pictures attributed to Pennsylvania furnaces date from 1741 to 1749, a period of only eight years if we except two extremely crude examples done in 1760. Comparatively few Bible stories were illustrated on stoveplates cast in America: twenty-three were from the Old Testament, and only ten from the New Testament. Neither the Nativity nor the Passion was represented. The most popular subjects were the Miracle of the Oil (2 Kings 4:1–7) in ten versions, and the Miracle at Cana (John 2:1–11) in eleven versions. These two events often decorate the same stove.

The only known eighteenth-century Pennsylvania stove patternmaker was Hen Snyder (1722–1767). All other designers of the cast-iron plates of this era are anonymous, so that there is still much speculation about them.

2652 *Franklin stove, following the inventor's plans, was not made during his lifetime. This design in the Adam style shows festooned decoration with the heads of Franklin and George Washington, made c. 1800–1810. Photograph* **2653** *Fireplace backs were cast in decorative patterns; this shows a very ornate handling of acanthus-leafed centers, with oak and acorn meanders.* **2654** *Fireplace iron casting in the Dumbarton House, c. 1790. Photograph* **2655–2659** *Forged wrought-iron hardware made in the eighteenth century in eastern Pennsylvania. The "double dragon" designs are shown in 2657 and 2658. Conestoga wagon toolbox-lid hardware is shown in 2659*

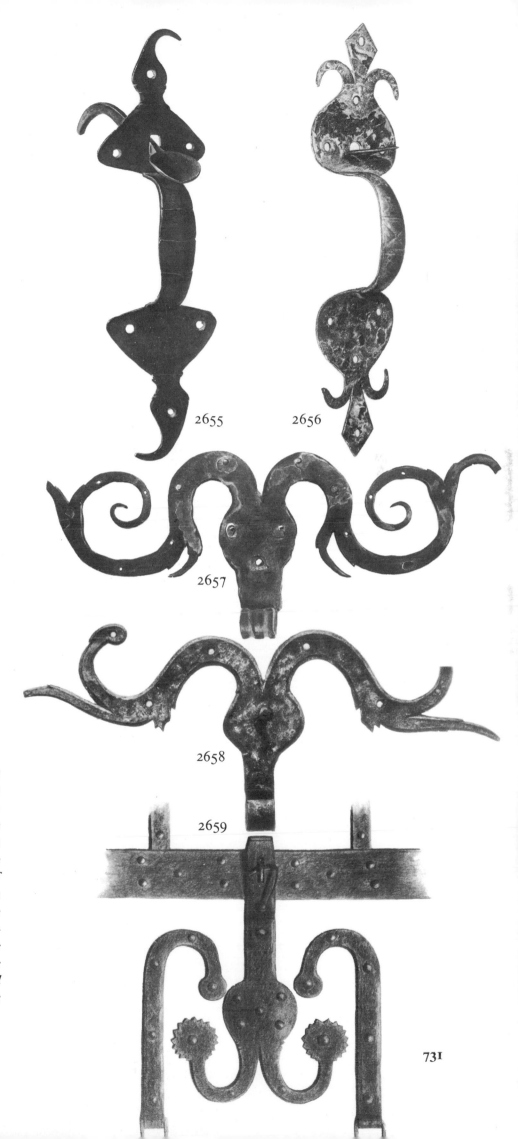

2655   2656

2657

2658

2659

731

2660

2660 *The stark simplicity of this Shaker room shows austerity carried to the point of fanaticism. Shunning all suggestion of decoration as an invitation to pleasurable experience, the Shakers fashioned every chair, table, bedspread, and cabinet to combine "strength, sprightliness, and modest beauty." Restraint is a characterizing feature, exemplified by the Brethren's rocking chair made about 1830 in New Lebanon, New York, the largest and most important Shaker establishment. The cast-iron stove is in marked contrast to the ornate products of contemporary foundries of that era. A long dining table, the built-in drawers, and closets are also consistently plain. The Millenial Laws of the sect directed that "floors in the dwelling houses, if stained at all, should be of a reddish-yellow," traces of which still show on the bare floors*

2661 *This unusual small table exhibits some slight deviation from the Shaker simplicity in the turned beadings on the pedestal and in the form of the tripod legs*

2661

Purity of Form ...
the Shaker Credo

UNCTIONALISM DECREES that any article shall be designed according to the purpose it is meant to fulfill, and by the same token eschews ornament as a disingenuous effort to conceal honest structure. Acting on these principles, the Shakers made a rare contribution to American design. Their furniture shows a most revealing insight into pure form, underlined by their belief that the utmost beauty lies in harmony, regularity, and order.

The communal group called the Shakers, originally the Shaking Quakers, were properly known as the United Society of Believers in Christ's Second Appearing. The sect was founded in the 1760s by Ann Lee of Manchester, England. In 1774 the founder and a small group of followers emigrated to America, where they first settled near Albany, New York. Despite many hardships, the sect prospered after the Revolution; within a few years of its founding, it boasted some eighteen

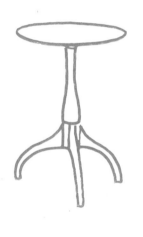

communities scattered throughout Maine, Massachusetts, Connecticut, New Hampshire, New York, Ohio, and Kentucky. The early converts to Shakerism came mainly from poor and simple folk. As their numbers increased, the Shakers had to depend on their own ingenuity and skill to fill the need for communal dwellings, barns, workshops, and mills. Before they could start to build, they had to fell trees in the forest, learn the properties of the different woods, and dam streams for waterpower to run their sawmills. They were fortunate in having wood in abundance and variety. The greater part of the built-in furniture—cupboards, chests of drawers, shelves, and wardrobes—was made of pine, which was easy to work and durable. After pine the wood most commonly used for furniture was hard, or rock, maple. There were also the so-called fruitwoods: cherry, pear, and apple. Cherry was favored for tabletops because it took a beautiful and lasting polish. Rock maple was the standard wood for slender articles that had to bear the strain of continuous use—pegs for the pegboard, spools, bobbins, and reels in the workshops, and drawer knobs—and also for posts, slats, rungs, and chair legs. Ash and hickory were valuable for the making of curved pieces. They are the "bending" woods, easily steamed to any shape. An example of the results of skillful steaming and bending, as practiced by the Shakers, was an oval box fabricated of two kinds of wood: pine for the top and bottom, and maple, cut to the thinness of an eighth of an inch, for the rounded sides. These boxes came in many sizes and were usually sold in nests of six or twelve.

The Shakers made both built-in and movable pieces of furniture. The built-in pieces became an integral part of the architectural scheme of the interiors: conceived in stark, simple terms, flush with wall surfaces, and designed to give maximum storage efficiency. Their movable furniture may be divided into two categories: those pieces intended for membership use in the dwelling houses and churches, and those built for the workshops, including spinning wheels, looms, cobblers' benches, and worktables of various kinds. But when the term "Shaker furniture" is used today, it usually refers to tables, bedsteads, benches, and especially chairs.

Shaker chairs were outstanding for their lightness, durability, and graceful beauty. The chairs had to be light because they were hung from pegs on the wall moldings whenever the floors were cleared for religious ceremonies. Like the tables and benches, the very earliest chairs were painted or stained a dark red. Later, the preference was for light stains and varnishes, which allowed the grain of the wood to show its natural beauty. No veneers or heavy lacquers were ever used; veneer was considered a sinful deceit and was strictly taboo. The earliest chair seats were rush, splint, plaited straw, or leather. Perhaps the single most distinguishing mark of the Shaker chair is the delicate finial at the top of each back post. These finials, like stylized pine cones, formed perfect extremities for the slender frames. Although they differed slightly from one community to another, they were always in harmony with the chair frame.

Shaker beds were very simple, hardly more

than cots. They were three feet wide, had short headboards and sometimes shorter footboards, all painted green, and were equipped with large wooden rollers. The "retiring rooms" were often fitted with rocking chairs or a variation called a "tilting chair," which was invented at New Lebanon, New York, about 1825; this afforded a pleasant tilting motion with no danger of slipping. The Shakers were probably the first people in this country to produce and use the rocking chair on a large scale. Intended originally for aged and infirm sisters and brethren, it was not long before rocking chairs were assigned to every retiring room, evidence that Shaker asceticism did not exclude some modicum of comfort. Rockers were made both with and without armrests, but followed no fixed pattern. They may be arbitrarily classified into mushroom-post, scrolled-arm, rolled-arm, cushion-rail, and sewing rockers. The mushroom post, used almost exclusively in the later Shaker chairs and rockers, was also common at an early period. At first the wide, gently crested, flat-bottomed mushrooms were turned in the same piece with the rest of the front post; later on, the mushroom was turned separately and attached by a hole bored into the arm post. As the Shaker rocker continued to grow in popularity, there were serious questions concerning its proper place in that inflexible society. During the great revival of 1840, one Philemon Stewart asked, "How comes it about that there are so many rocking chairs used? Is the rising generation going to be able to keep the way of God, by seeking after ease?"

It has been charged that since the Shakers used simple forms inherited from the plain country style of early New England, they originated no new designs and cannot be considered a creative people. In a limited sense this is true; theirs was a gift of simplification and refinement. By discarding all unnecessary artifice and embellishment, the Shakers reduced these early designs to their essentials of form and proportion and achieved distinctly beautiful results. The conformity to an accepted design was one of the basic tenets of the Shaker approach.

Although an individual's efforts were subordinate to the common welfare, it cannot be said that the Shakers stifled personal expression. As a matter of fact, individual development was encouraged. When it was seen that a member was proficient in a specific craft, that worker was permitted complete freedom of performance. Many Shaker cabinetmakers were known by name even though they were not permitted to sign their pieces. When the Shaker communities were enjoying their greatest prosperity, in the period roughly from 1820 to 1870, the master craftsmen produced an amazing assortment of "sprightly" furniture. Personalities of exceptional skill, among them James Farnum, Gilbert Avery, John Lockwood, George Wickersham, Benjamin Youngs, Thomas Fisher, and Robert Wagon, attuned to the spirit of simplicity, designed and executed hundreds of fine, unpretentious pieces. These were either copied exactly by apprentices or were altered to fit particular needs: the master craftsman became the designer and executed the prototype, which

735

2662

2664

736

2663

2662–2666 *Since the Shakers believed that "True Gospel simplicity . . . naturally leads to plainness in all things," it affected every design, whether in architecture, furniture, or textiles. The winding stairway,* **2662,** *exhibits this restraint, its graceful lines merely tracing the form of its architecture. Cabinets and closets invariably had wooden knobs, never metal. The mushroom rocker,* **2666,** *with its four slats and cone finials, became the archetype widely copied in many areas. To the Shakers must go credit for popularizing the rocking chair. The bedstead,* **2665,** *is very similar to a type to be found in the Zoar community, in Ohio*

2665

2666

was reproduced in such quantity that mail-order sales became possible in the 1880s.

Religious fervor and a high degree of dedication motivated every member in the pursuance of his daily work. Whether the excellence they attained is attributable to religious impulse or was the result of the true craftsman's attitude to the task in hand, the end product carried its own reward. Surely, the perfecting of utility and the designing of forms so pure were made possible only by a high quality of skill, technical ability which, in the words of Joseph Conrad, embraced "honesty and grace and rule in an elevated and clear sentiment, not altogether utilitarian, which may be called the honor of labor."

2667

2668

2669

738

2670

2671

2667–2671 *Efficient use of storage space followed strictly the precepts of Mother Ann, the founder, that "care and management of temporal things" was a cardinal principle. It followed that domestic order and neatness were the individual responsibility of every occupant of a communal dwelling. Order necessitated the construction of a great number of chests, cases of drawers, cupboards, and closets, as all bedclothes, clothing, textiles, and utensils were required to be put out of sight. Built-in drawers and overhead cupboard space were architecturally incorporated for maximum efficiency,* **2668**. *The white porcelain knobs on the secretary,* **2671**, *distinguished storage space for smaller knickknacks*

2672

2673

2674

740

2675

2676

2672–2677 *The pie safe,* **2672,** *shows twenty panels of tin, simply perforated to permit ventilation. The sewing table,* **2673,** *has delicately shaped legs. The large dining table,* **2674,** *has a pine top four feet wide and trestles made of birch; frequently such tables measured twenty feet long. The crib, shown in* **2677,** *appears in both Shaker and Zoar communities*

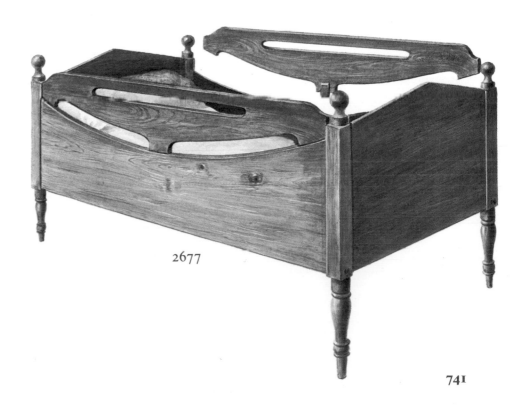

2677

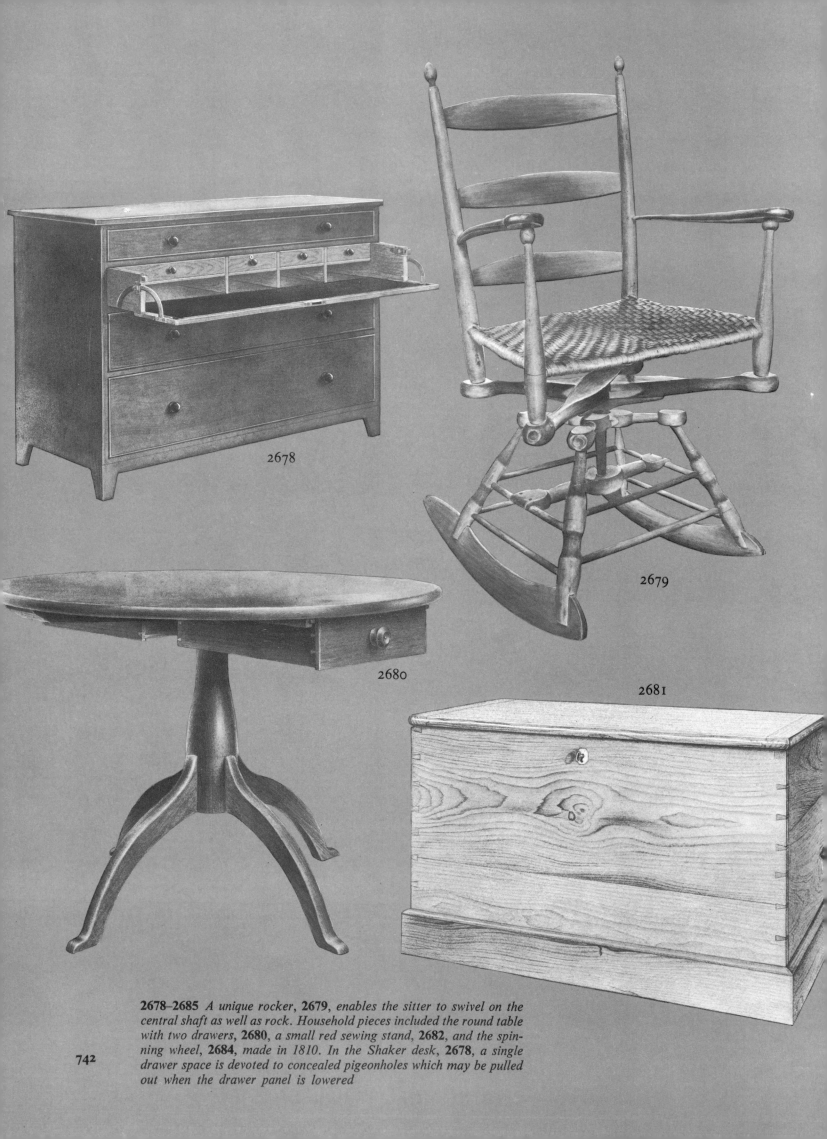

2678

2679

2680

2681

2678–2685 *A unique rocker,* **2679,** *enables the sitter to swivel on the central shaft as well as rock. Household pieces included the round table with two drawers,* **2680,** *a small red sewing stand,* **2682,** *and the spinning wheel,* **2684,** *made in 1810. In the Shaker desk,* **2678,** *a single drawer space is devoted to concealed pigeonholes which may be pulled out when the drawer panel is lowered*

2682

2683

2684

2685

2686

2687

2688

2689

The Separatists of Zoar

HISTORY RECORDS some three hundred experiments in communal living in America during the past three centuries. For the most part, they were based on religious rather than economic tenets. One of the longest-lived and most successful communities was founded by a band of Pietists in Tuscarawas County, Ohio, in 1817. Aided by wealthy and sympathetic Quakers and led by Jacob Bimiler, they built a little village which still stands, almost untouched by time.

Bimiler was a strange genius who combined the position of religious leader with that of business agent. He was quick to see the market for the group's excess products in the surrounding countryside. Bimiler sold the community's farm products, developed the mineral resources of the land, and eventually operated the general store, which carried practically everything needed in a frontier settlement. He did not hesitate to hire outside artisans and craftsmen for extra help in the community. The combination of agriculture and industry brought fame and fortune to the town of Zoar. One result of the economic success was a commodious community building known as King's House. This twenty-one-

2686 *Plank chair showing influence of traditional German peasant furniture of the seventeenth and and eighteenth centuries* 2687 *Perpetual calendar with movable dials indicating in German not only the days and months but also the times of sunrise and sunset and the fixed holidays. Hand-painted decorations on wood show flowers and castles reminiscent of native Germany* 2688 *In this Zoar furnace floriated panels are set into sides and front facing, repeated on tinplate below, 1835* 2689 *Frame for baptismal certificate built up of spool sections, c. 1817–37* 2689A *Butter mold of five-branched swirl design* 2690 *Thread holder, made near Zoar, Ohio, c. 1825–45*

2690

2691

2692

room brick structure, today a museum, was erected in 1843, and Bimiler died ten years later. He left no adequate successor, but the well-established industries continued to run along without interruption. In 1898, no longer able to compete with modern methods and tired of the rigid discipline, the members finally disbanded. At the time of dissolution, property valued at over a million dollars was divided among the hundred and thirty-six surviving members.

The Zoar craftsmen brought with them a strong German tradition, which manifested itself in furniture design and in the decorative arts and crafts. Although they were separated from their neighbors by custom and religion and were admonished to keep to themselves, they still allowed outsiders to influence them. The well-defined Germanic style of their earliest work became diffused, and from this cross-breeding there resulted a selection of motifs and styles thoroughly typical of Midwestern, mid-nineteenth century America.

Zoar furniture styles ranged from sixteenth-century European designs to walnut parlor pieces of the 1880s. The first furniture made at Zoar was purely Germanic in its derivation: plank-seat chairs, large wardrobes, and small cupboards. The hanging cupboards, painted a gray-blue color, were a favorite form which, according to tradition, concealed ornamental glass and china behind heavily decorated doors. Later the furniture showed traces of prevailing period styles, such as German Biedermeier, Hepplewhite, Sheraton, and American Empire. These were attributable to such outside cabinetmakers as John Leser, George Hagney, and I. Fritz, whose names were accurately recorded in daybooks from 1836 to 1858.

It is interesting to observe that the work of outsiders was encouraged for purely economic reasons. Furniture made for members was severely simple and often rather heavy, with slight German accents. Tables were seldom the drop-leaf type, so popular throughout the Midwest; they were more likely to be tavern tables with pinned-on tops. Stands, chests of

2691 *Bonnet cabinet of cherry with decorated panels, made in Zoar, Ohio, c. 1836* **2692** *Painted and decorated Zoarite chair, c. 1860–70* **2693** *Black walnut hanging cabinet, known in the Zoar Schwabian dialect as* Haube-Kaeschtle, *1836* **2694** *Rocker made in Zoar, with shaped seat and arrow spindles*

drawers, beds, "kitchen Windsor" chairs, and slat-back chairs were all made for use at Zoar. Cherry was the favorite wood, but poplar or tulipwood and some walnut, pine, maple, and hickory were also utilized. Rather than the traditional German painted decoration, the craftsmen preferred red or a gray-blue color which was often given the appearance of wood grain.

Over thirty-five trades and crafts were practiced in the Zoar community, including printing and binding. The iron foundry, the woolen mill, and the pottery were the most significant commercial enterprises. The new settlers were quick to avail themselves of the good clay on their property; surprisingly, their first products were roof tiles of the North European type. Their pottery, for the most part, was unglazed redware. Some examples show soft orange-red clay under a light coating of glaze, and some were coated with yellow slip before glazing. Decoration was simple, usually plain incised lines. Less often there was slip decoration, thinly applied in contrast to the heavy slip of the Pennsylvania potters. A few pieces of Rockingham and yellowware are ascribed to Zoar; the hard, stony brown glaze characteristic of much Ohio pottery was also used.

Many other trades were carried on at Zoar. Conrad Dienman, an expert woodturner, probably made many of the spinning wheels sold in the general store. A wagonmaker, a cooper, and a watchmaker all worked in the community and served outside customers. A tin shop, operated by John Moffatt from 1837 to 1860 or later, made tea- and coffeepots, buckets, dippers, measures, funnels, boxes, candle molds, covered cans, and some attractive cookie cutters. Most of this toleware was unadorned; the general store was interested in quick sales at modest prices.

The quality of Zoar workmanship was always honest. The simple products lacked the purity of the traditional Shaker output and the decorated works did not display the flair and originality the Pennsylvanians demonstrated. Even so, Zoar craftsmanship remains an example of the results which can be achieved in a well-knit community which is sustained by group discipline and sensitive to neighboring influences in the mainstream of American folk arts and crafts.

2693

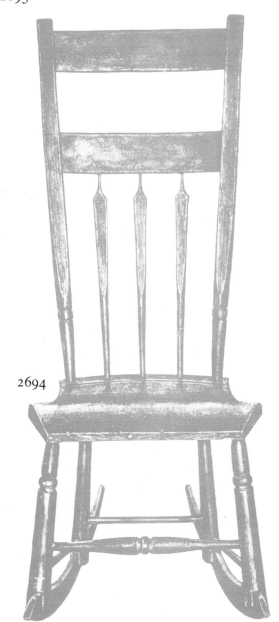

2694

2695

Icons & Images of the Santeros

2696

FRANCISCO DE CORONADO first explored the Southwest in 1540, pushing northward from Mexico in search of the fabled Seven Cities of Cibola. Many other Spanish conquistadores followed in this period of exploration, but not until the closing years of the sixteenth century was any attempt made at colonization. In 1598, accompanied by a group of missionaries and colonists, Juan de Oñate established the first permanent settlement in the Southwest. By 1610 Santa Fe had become the capital of the region that encompassed Arizona, New Mexico, Colorado, and western Texas.

The territory of New Spain extended all the way from Mexico and Central America, including the hundreds of Caribbean Islands, up through that region. In the course of time the frontiers pushed eastward to include all of Texas and westward to cover all of California. Although a settlement had been established in St. Augustine in 1565, there had been no large-scale attempt at colonization in Florida and two hundred years of occupation failed to leave any permanent cultural imprint. In the Spanish Southwest, however, the more serious drive had a lasting effect upon the arts and crafts of the area. After Oñate's conquest the Pueblos lived in virtual servitude for some eighty years. They finally rebelled in 1680, causing the massacre of about four hundred Spaniards. Their freedom was short-lived; in 1692, De Vargas crushed their revolt with a fierce tyranny. The battles of those days wiped out early Spanish Colonial artifacts; hardly a trace of the decorative crafts has survived from

2695 Retablo *painted on wood with gesso ground, dated 1783. San Jose, California* **2696** Saint George and the Dragon, *carved of pine by Celso Gallegos, c. 1920. Like the work of the earlier* santeros, *such fanciful figures and subjects in relief were used not only to decorate graves but also as* santos *for the home*

the period antedating 1700. After the reconquest of the area, the mission of San Xavier del Bac was established and became the first outpost in Arizona; San Antonio emerged as the center of the small colony in Texas. The last thrust of the Spanish empire was the string of Franciscan missions set up by Padre Junipero Serra. In 1769 he founded his first mission in San Diego, and in 1823 his last. In 1821 Mexico's break with Spain encouraged secularization and effectively destroyed the mission system. Thereafter, large numbers of American settlers began to arrive in Texas, coming by covered wagons which rolled westward from Missouri on the Santa Fe Trail. By mid-century the great rush was on to the California goldfields; the entire Southwest territory had become part of the United States, ending three centuries of Spanish domination.

The California missions became citadels of artistic culture, as well as centers for the conversion of the Indians and protective presidios aimed at thwarting British and Russian encroachment. Each mission was a self-sustaining community with grainfields and orchards, a water-supply system, and quarters for Indians and soldiers. The natives were taught weaving, pottery, tanning, soap making, and the production of other marketable commodities. Every effort was made by the padres to make the Indians self-reliant, but they were slow to adopt new ways. By the time of the Mexican Revolution, the period of cultural development had not been long enough for distinctive new art forms to flourish. Thus, the California heritage became an admixture of Mexican art, local workmanship based on Mexican and European designs, and a remarkable blending of Spanish and Indian elements.

In contrast to the coastal regions, where intercourse between settlements could be conducted by crude, ox-drawn carts along El Camino Real or by sailing vessels visiting the important harbor towns, the New Mexican

areas were markedly separated from Mexican culture; distances were vast and the terrain forbidding. To the south, the Spanish superstructure was simply imposed upon the Pueblo Indian base which was already well established when the Spanish colonists came. These *pueblos* (towns and villages) were situated mainly in northern New Mexico along the upper Rio Grande; consequently, the first settlements sprang up in this region. The Indians' communal way of life was sedentary, agrarian. The Indians were also skilled in weaving and basketmaking. In these isolated mountain hamlets, after a long period of germination, the folk art of New Mexico developed. Some Mexican influences on the Indian culture can be detected, particularly in sculpture and wood carving.

Historically, the crafts and folk arts of the Spanish Colonial Southwest may be divided as follows: the period of Spanish rule dating from the reconquest of New Mexico to the Mexican Independence (1692–1821), the Mexican Republic (1823–48), and the American period, commencing when these territories came into the Union (1848). It was the Spanish missions that first gave the style of the Southwest its essential character. In the ranch period, distinguished by the formation of the great landed estates of California (1820–50), no more new missions were added to the chain. Separated from the control of the Church, they lost their influence and fell into decay. The Indians who had attached themselves to the mission communities were dispossessed and became peons or cowboys. The craftsmen who survived practiced outside the church or mission community, and with the coming of industry their folk art gradually disappeared.

At the very outset of the Spanish infiltration, architecture and crafts were brought to the Southwest from Mexico by the Franciscan priests. Under their tutelage local workers learned new techniques: how to work in

metals, principally silver and tin; how to carve and build in stone; and how to use paints in the European manner. All of the teachings of the priesthood were designed to inculcate the spirit and fervor of the Church, and thus the *santero* school of painting, wood carving, and sculpture was born. The *santo* (saint) was a holy image. To Spanish-speaking New Mexicans *un santo* means any religious image, whether in wood, stone, metal, plaster, painting, or print. In recent years the New Mexicans have appropriated the term to mean indigenous folk images. A maker or repairer of *santos* is called a *santero*, and his products fall into two categories: pictures painted on wood panels, called *retablos*, and figures carved of wood, covered with a gesso base, and painted, called *bultos*.

California missions possessed numbers of paintings imported from Mexico, where they had been done in the European manner; in New Mexico oil canvases were virtually unknown. The native *santeros* were taught by the priests to paint directly on panels of cottonwood or pine which were first treated with gesso. Only a small number of these *retablo* paintings were signed. Father García, serving in New Mexico (1747–79), Father Pereyro (1798–1818), José Aragón (1822–35), and Father Molleño (1828–45) are a few whose works are identifiable by signature or stylistic mannerisms. The earlier *retablo* paintings were the inspired oeuvre of the priests themselves and were used to decorate church walls or altarpieces. The paintings were characterized by lively gestures and expressive features. Although the native *santeros* attempted to follow in the footsteps of their instructors, their works were less animated. No longer designed as statues, carved figures became images for the home; each adobe had its patron saint. Through stylization these figures assumed a simplicity of form and a naive monumentality.

The native *santero*, after learning his craft

from a teacher-priest, usually decided to sell his *santos* for a livelihood. He traveled from town to town and, much like his distant cousin the Yankee peddler, offered his wares at the household door as bringers of good luck. To the native the image was the source of supernatural power that would heal the sick, cure the lame, and insure a bountiful harvest. There were also amateur *santeros* who did the work as an exercise in religious devotion, one that was certain to yield blessings.

The *bulto*, a small free-standing statuette of a single saint or group, was carved in the round. Made of cottonwood roots more often than pine, the *bulto* served for daily reverence, general decoration, and as a talisman. If the posture called for outstretched arms or limbs in other extended positions, these were carved separately and pegged into the body, following which the body was smoothly covered with gesso ground and painted. For realistic drapery, cotton folds were applied to the figure after being dipped into wet gesso. The earlier figures, antedating 1800, followed the Mexican Baroque style. The so-called Cordova *bultos*, named after the village of their origin, are thought to be the work of José Rafael Aragon, a *santero* working in the period of 1830–50. These figures are tall and elegant, with faces finely chiseled and clearly colored. The Mora type of *bulto*, named for the Mora river and valley district, shows highly stylized modeling and dates from about the Civil War period.

The timeless aspect of the culture of the Southwest stands out in the architectural base which the Spanish settlers inherited from the Indians. The Pueblos had been building multi-storied apartment dwellings since about 700 A.D. Some were tucked away in cave openings like the Cliff House near Flagstaff; others, like the North House of Taos, stood on open, sun-baked plains. The Spaniards did not destroy this Indian way of life but adopted it, using their own tools and techniques to create a

2697

2698

2699

2700

2701

2697–2704 Santos *and* bultos *were often carved and polychromed by* traveling santeros, *who sold the religious images in remote villages. Since every home needed guardianship, the household altar was graced by a little statuette before which prayers were offered* **2698** *Retablo dedicated to San Procopio by an unknown painter in the style of Miguel Aragón, c. 1830–50*

2702

2703

2704

2705

2706

blend that became the unique style of the region. Indeed, tools and implements were among the rarest of commodities. There was no real progress in the building arts until the settlers arrived with planes, saws, bits, and augers. Further advances were made when the railroad was extended to this area.

Adobe, which is mud mixed from the clay-and-gypsum desert soil and baked by the sun, served as the universal building agent. By piling up layers of adobe, the Indians built their homes of many stories to make a *pueblo*, or town. The Spaniards improved this crude method by mixing straw with the adobe and baking it into bricks. On their cattle ranches they limited themselves to single stories of wide adobe construction, which developed into the contemporary ranch style.

2707

2708

2709

2710

The generously proportioned plaster walls of the missions presented an opportunity for the Indian painters, who covered them lavishly with religious themes—the Crucifixion and stories of the saints—adding ancient Indian symbols and using the exuberant colors developed in their ceremonial paintings. Mission art work was a unique fusion of European architecture with the kind of crude Indian motif that appears in the petrographs, or rock paintings, of the region. The artists also produced large easel paintings, such as the Stations of the Cross, which are exceptional in regional folk art.

2705 Retablo *of a type common to New Mexico, painted between 1750 and 1850. A pine board covered with gesso, then painted in tempera* **2707** Bulto *from the church at Ranchos de Taos, made between 1830 and 1850. Clearly copied from a print or small painting, as evidenced by the artist's inability to cope with the upper ends of drapery* **2706, 2708, 2709** *Pine or cottonwood crosses used as grave markers show great variety and ingenuity in the silhouette designs. Decorative effects were obtained in zigzag cuts in the outlines, rarely with carvings on the flat surfaces. In 2708 there are appliquéd ornaments of tin and the wooden surfaces are decorated* **2710** Retablo *of the Holy Ghost painted in the region of the Rio Grande valley* **2711** *The Immaculate Conception was declared the principal doctrine of all Spanish possessions, including those in the New World. This carved and painted* bulto *was made in New Mexico, 1830–50*

2711

755

2712

2713

2714

2712-2717 *Painted chests, especially the front and top panels, were often gaily decorated with floral designs, figures, and tableaux suggestive of fiesta pageantry. Bright colors, exuberant figures, and lush vegetation combined to convey the lively Latin temperament. The general feeling of design of these chest panels, painted in New Mexico in the first half of the nineteenth century, is derivative of an influence traced to Mexico, in the area of Chihuahua* **2714** *Embroidery in which floral and leaf forms are handsomely designed and competently executed*

2715

2716

2717

2718

2718–2721 *Representative of a group of about forty chests similarly painted and decorated, these display amazing freshness and colorful vitality. The pictorial theme might be a handful of dragoons in boats, odd-shaped and without oars,* 2718, 2720, *a pair of tropical birds in gay plumage,* 2721, *or a pair of animals of uncertain species. But always the background areas are completely covered with rosettes, lunettes, and an assortment of rich foliage rendered in bright hues that delight the eye*

2719

2720

2721

759

2722

2723

2722 Santo *enshrined in an enclosed setting. Made in New Mexico, nineteenth century* **2723** *Ceremonial candlestick of carved native pine, polychromed over gesso base. Made in the Spanish-Californian Mission style, c. 1815* **2724–2727** *The chest on stand,* caja en mesita, **2724,** *was often massively proportioned for a large adobe house. Carvings of inset panels are identified with the style of Taos. The base shows the pronounced sawtooth motif characteristic of effects obtained with limited tools, c. 1870. In* **2725,** *corner stiles are simply carved as legs. Hasps and hinges of wrought iron are of local origin, though often these were imported from Mexico; made in northern New Mexico, c. 1850. Trinket box,* **2726,** *has deep carving on all sides, buckskin hinges, c. 1860. The small chest,* **2727,** *made in the vicinity of Taos, c. 1800, is decorated with fanciful scrolls and abstract forms*

2724

Furniture &

Furnishings

of the

Southwest

2725

2726

2727

2728

2731

2729

2728–2730, 2733 *The colcha is a typical form of New Mexican needlework in wool using a long stitch crossed at a 45-degree angle by a short holding stitch. The term* colcha *is derived from the classical Spanish for "stitch"; the New Mexican quilt is called a* colchone. *Embroidered wool bedcovers date from the 1840s and represent a form of folk needlecraft. Characteristic of this type are the florets and nosegays of carnations, pomegranates, and other flowers and foliage, done in vibrant colors of warmth and gaiety. An enlarged detail from the corner of 2729 is shown in 2733. 2731 Bedspread of cotton embroidery showing crewel stitch on closely woven canvas, c. 1870–80 2734, 2735 California Indian basketry has been considered the finest of its type ever woven. The designs combine motifs like blocks, diamonds, chevrons, and, as in 2735, conventionalized renderings of the Spanish royal coat of arms, castles, and lions. An inscription woven into the border tells of its maker, Anna Maria Marta of the Mission of Saint Bonaventure. The basket is woven in the usual Indian fashion of coils covered with rush and sewn together*

2730

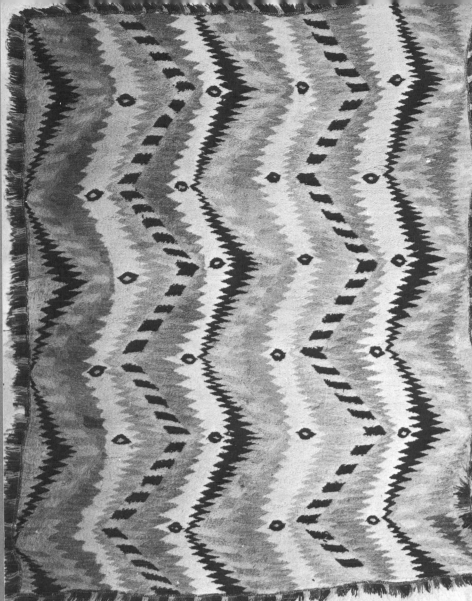

2732

2733

2734

2735

763

2736

2737

2738

2736–2740 *Chairs of the Southwest, while of definite Spanish influence, with carved details and leatherwork embossed and covered with large brass heads, were primitive in their lines. They follow rigid construction, using square posts as legs and flat, unupholstered seats. Stretchers are either carved or plain. The monk's chair,* **2740,** *was not designed for comfort; the back splat shows the sawtooth design found in many of the plainer examples of this region. The long bench,* **2737,** *also shows the simple saw-cut motifs, a most primitive attempt at introducing decoration* **2741** *Carved and painted redwood cabinet, with wrought-iron hinges. Made by an Indian craftsman at the Mission San Juan Bautista* **2742, 2744** *The picture frame,* **2742,** *and the wall sconce,* **2744,** *show a type of decorative tinware indigenous to the Southwest, derivative of the finer silverware of similar design. However, instead of chasing and tooling for ornamentation, the worker in tin used punches, embossing, and piercing to obtain results* **2743** *Lock plate features the double eagle. Its inspiration could be both Mexican and American*

2739

2740

2741

2742

2743

2744

765

2745

2746

2747

2748

766

2749

2750

2751

2745–2752 *An array of furniture of the Spanish Southwest demonstrates the paucity of working implements. Chests and tables were square and squatty, with a massive quality of heavy workmanship. Often the introduction of a decorative stretcher or apron, as in* **2747** *and* **2748***, results in a scallop or sawtooth design as one of expediency. The monstrance,* **2745***, achieves a decorative note from simple cutouts and drilled holes and the addition of moldings. The turned candlestick,* **2749***, is brightly colored in orange with cool greens and blues. A more ornate treatment above the opening of the confessional,* **2751***, attempts to glorify, with simple means, the special purposes of this religious piece. The mission chimes,* **2752***, have a homespun quality; the same may be said of the candelabra,* **2746***, made of tin with arms twisted in all directions*

2752

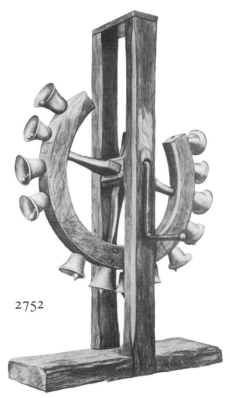

767

2753

2753 Branding Scene, *painted by S. Morgan Bryan. Kennedy Galleries, New York* **2754** *Proprietary marks made on various parts of the calf's hide by knife cuts and slashes*

Heraldry of the Range

2754

LIKE SO MANY OTHER TRADITIONS and customs in the cattle industry, branding can be traced back to the arrival of the Spanish conquistador Cortés. When Cortés and Pizarro were building a new empire that stretched from Mexico to Peru, Cortés branded slaves and animal stock alike with the sign of the Three Christian Crosses. Spaniards had traditionally put their house marks on everything they owned since medieval times, and the brand was simply a declaration of ownership. From this simple assertion of authority there developed a system of marking untold millions of cattle, a complicated code of laws and regulations, and a fascinating array of tools and techniques.

Brands were placed on livestock with a stamp iron or running iron soon after calfing time, when the young heifers had to be marked and counted. It was a dirty, dusty business, requiring the combined efforts of a half dozen cowhands to rope and hold the cantankerous beasts, tend the fire in which the irons were heated, and burn the mark into the tender young hide.

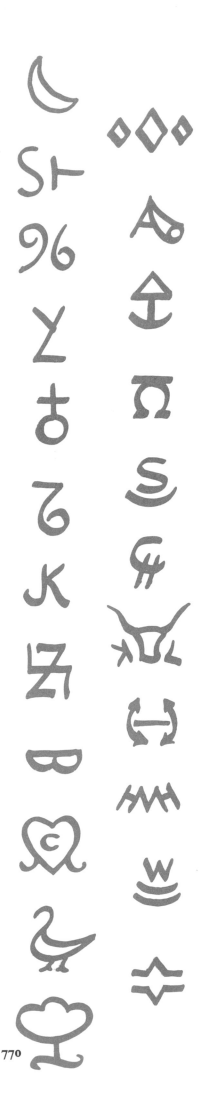

After years of violations and cattle theft, the ranchers decided that some form of legal registration was necessary, so the brand of each ranch was entered in an official brand book at the county seat. Even so, it was difficult to create a design that could not be altered. The brand might be composed of any combination of letters, numerals, or abstract shapes. Some of the more unusual included the Walking R, Rocking H, Lazy Y, Cut and Slash, Forked Lightning, Man in the Moon, and Crazy Three. Literally thousands of these were registered across the West.

To make a brand the ranch blacksmith would turn to his forge and deftly twist a few small bits of iron into the required shape, beating the joints into a single form and fixing it to a long poker handle. The stamp enabled the brander to burn the mark into the hide in a single operation.

When an animal was sold to another ranch the new owner placed his brand on it. To make the transfer legitimate, the original owner vented (from the Spanish *vender*, to sell) his brand—usually by burning a bar across it. The hide of the unfortunate horse or cow that had been sold a number of times began to resemble an informal brand directory or a well-traveled piece of luggage.

In later years, when leather became a more valuable commodity, the practice of defacing the hide declined. An elaborate system of earmarking was substituted, with slits and cuts devised in endless combinations. The extensive glossary of terms used to describe earmarks is a language that only the experienced rancher understands. Such descriptive words as "overslope," "swallow fork," "jingle bob," or "over-and-under bit" testify to the ingenuity of the cowhands in overcoming difficult assignments on the range.

2762

770

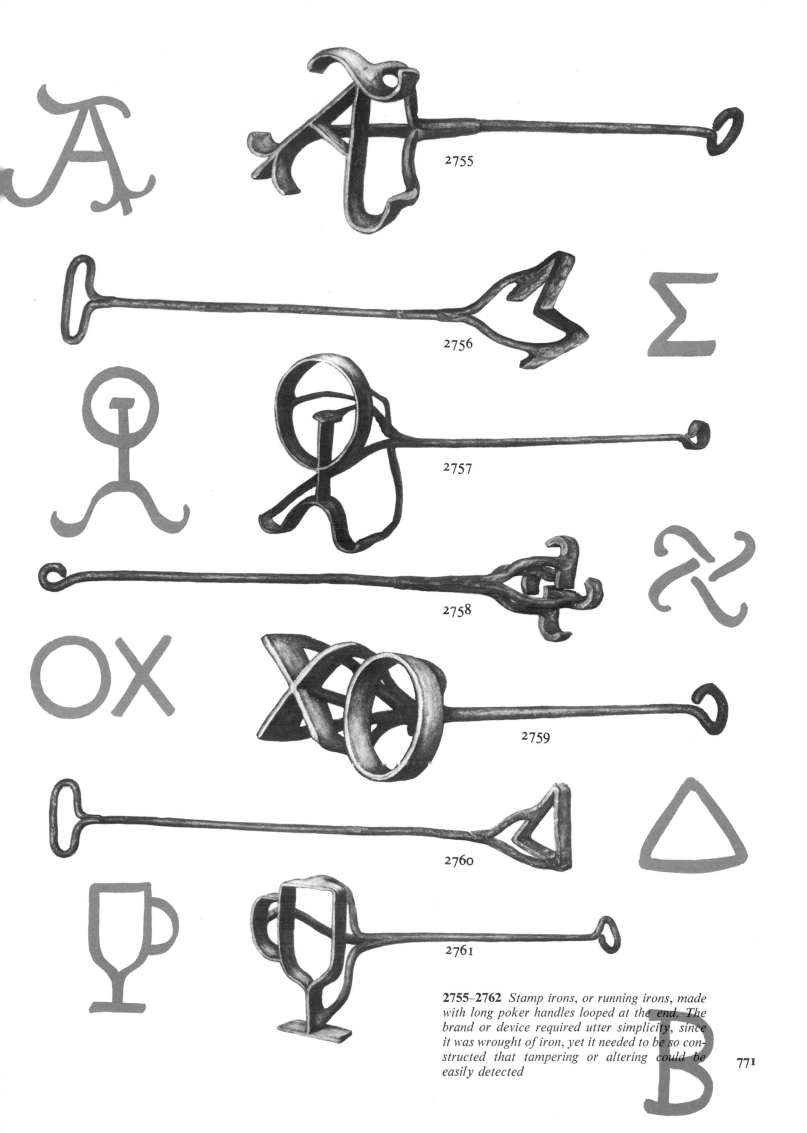

2755

2756

2757

2758

2759

2760

2761

2755–2762 *Stamp irons, or running irons, made with long poker handles looped at the end. The brand or device required utter simplicity, since it was wrought of iron, yet it needed to be so constructed that tampering or altering could be easily detected*

771

2763

Bridles, Bits & Spurs

2764

2765

I N THE RIDING gear of the cattleman hardly a square inch of the metal or leather surfaces is free from some form of decoration.

Like so many other Western traditions, this can be traced to Mexican practices and beyond that to origins in medieval Spain. During Spain's Golden Age, a style of extravagant decoration developed in which floral designs were freely interspersed with figures and animal motifs set in bold relief.

The trend toward unrestrained opulence reached its height during the Renaissance, and by the time Philip II ascended the throne in 1556 there was a positive lust for effusive ostentation. The plateresque style, distinguished by a richness of ornamentation suggestive of silver plate was the style of the day, and it was this love of embellishment that formed the heritage of every craftsman in the Southwest, whether he worked in iron, silver, or leather.

2763 *The hackamore bit is a prime tool, especially useful when taming or training a colt. Side pieces are often gaily decorated. This one features the female form in outline, brand marks on the silver crosspiece, and a serpent below. Bosal at top is of woven thongs* **2764, 2765** *Bridle bits forged of iron, including chain, links and tassels on crossbar*

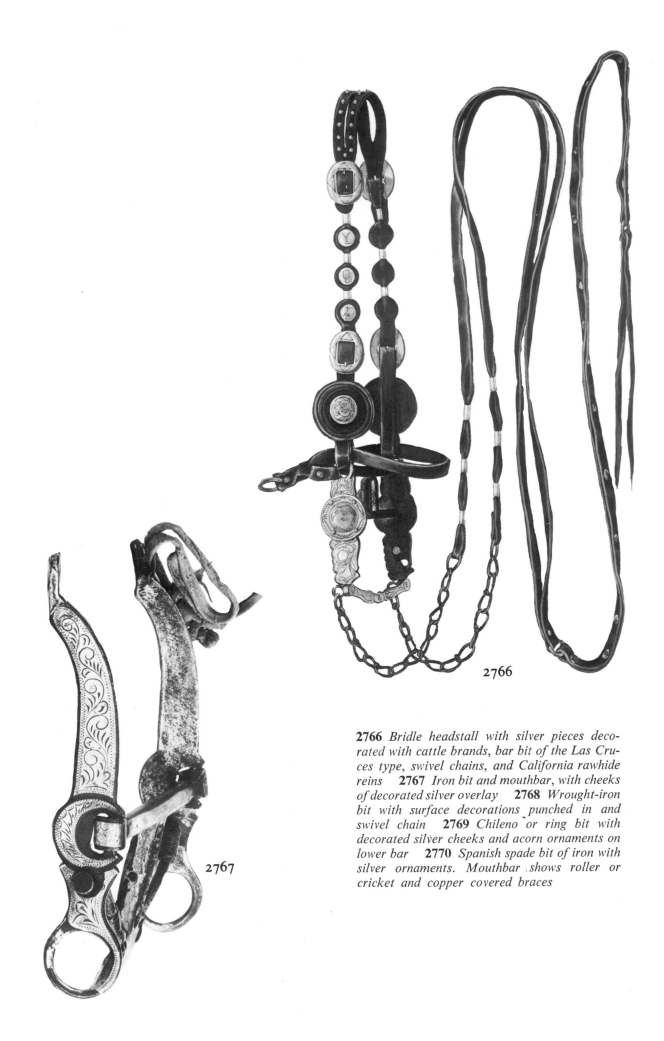

2766

2767

2766 *Bridle headstall with silver pieces decorated with cattle brands, bar bit of the Las Cruces type, swivel chains, and California rawhide reins* **2767** *Iron bit and mouthbar, with cheeks of decorated silver overlay* **2768** *Wrought-iron bit with surface decorations punched in and swivel chain* **2769** *Chileno or ring bit with decorated silver cheeks and acorn ornaments on lower bar* **2770** *Spanish spade bit of iron with silver ornaments. Mouthbar shows roller or cricket and copper covered braces*

The bridle headstall, or headgear of the horse, enabled the *caballero* to display all the skill and artistry of the craftsmen of his ranch. The many parts of the bridle—crownpiece, browband, throatlatch, cheekpiece—invited the decorative touches that lent glamour to the headpiece. The cheekpieces were ornamented with spots and *conchas* (shell-shaped disks of silver). Dangling chains, though noisy, were added because they were believed to provide entertainment for the horse. Bits offered the greatest opportunity for imaginative treatment, and an endless variety of fanciful designs that combined fine steel and silver were produced.

The spurs worn by all *rancheros* can be traced back to the ancient prod or pryck. From this simple pointed spur the revolving rowel developed. It was made in many forms from long, sharp-pointed stars to sawtooth and smoothly rounded rowels designed to inflict less pain on the horse. The spur shank, button, heel band, and heel chains were integral parts that could be richly embellished. The status of the horseman could be gauged by the amount of ornamentation on his boots and spurs as well as on his horse's saddle and bridle.

Every detail of the cowboy's equipment tended to the ornate rather than to functional simplicity, a tradition that continues to this day. The virile cowhand never disdained fancy clothes, and his chaps, belts, and hat were often encrusted with silver ornaments.

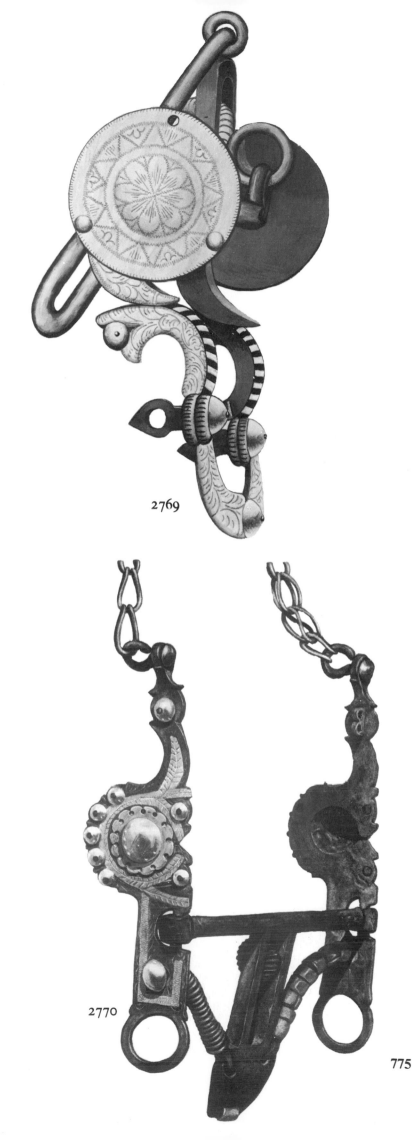

2769

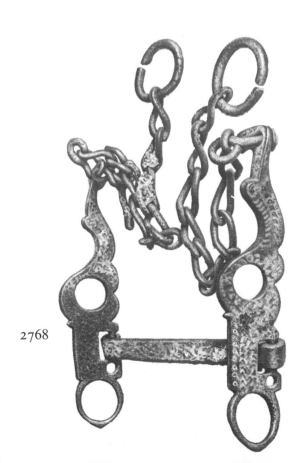

2768

2770

775

2771

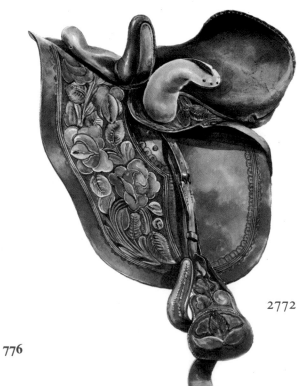

2771 Bronc on a Frosty Morn, *painted in 1898 by Charles Marion Russell. The setting is the Judith Basin, Montana, where Russell spent many of his early years as a cowpuncher* **2772** *Tooled-leather sidesaddle with rose and leaf decorations; seat and cantle feature stitched decorations*

2773 *Saddle with horn decorated with a star and the name "Whitby." Cantle of hand-tooling showing the initials "O W," side pouch with decorated lid, silver mounts, and tie strings*

2772

Tools & Trappings
of the Cowhands

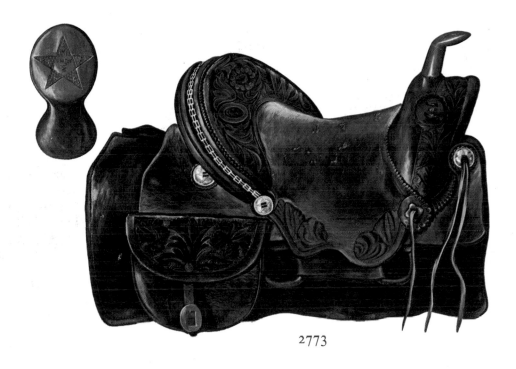

2773

CATTLE TENDING in the South-west dates from the early six-teenth century when the Spanish conquistadores under Hernando Cortés introduced longhorns into Mexico. The descendants of these early adventurers operated large estates known as *haciendas*, or, in the case of smaller operations, *ranchos*. The men employed on every ranch, large or small, to handle the cows were called *vaqueros*, meaning cowboys. (The American equivalent "buckaroo" is simply a corruption of the Spanish word.) Slowly the great herds drifted northward, where grazing conditions were superior. In Texas the herds were incredibly vast, and mustangs and cattle which ran wild could be had for the taking. Thus the classic cowboy of the Southwest was born of Mexican

tradition and American necessity. With him came all the Spanish terminology for cowboy gear and cattle herding, along with picaresque characters and legends of the Old West.

The accessories of the range and cattle tending, as well as the cowhand's personal accouterments, consisted of leather goods and ironware. The metalwork was wrought in simple, functional forms, yet, where practicable, these were made to yield an ornamental twist. Typical of the region's metalwork were: branding irons in many designs, since each ranch needed its own distinctive brand mark for quick identification of cattle; silver bridle bits, wrought with great delicacy and artistry in fanciful designs; steel stirrups, trimmed and overlaid with silver; steel spurs, often with mountings and other details of chased silver; and a great variety of wrought hardware—such as picket pins for tethering a horse—needed for use on the ranch. Thus an important place on every large ranch was the smith's shop, where there was not only constant shoeing to be done, but also the making of the hundred-and-one requisites of the range. In addition to the blacksmith's efforts, the local silversmith contributed his glistening bit to ornament the dull wrought-steel pieces. Working separately or as a team, these two craftsmen were responsible for all the hardware, plain or decorated, for which the Southwest was justly famous.

Pen and ink sketches of bronco busting by Edward Borein, from his book Borein's West

2774

2774 *Child's sidesaddle, c. 1820, by an unknown craftsman from Monterey, California. Handsomely embroidered in silk, the velvet-upholstered seat shows Diana, protectress of maidens, in a chariot drawn by two goats. The cornucopias embroidered on both sides are logical Neoclassical attributes, for this goddess was identified with fertility rites and was honored at harvest time. The border design and workmanship are of superior quality, suggesting older centers of the craft in Mexico* **2775** *Oxbow stirrup with American eagle in chased-silver mounting* **2776, 2777** *Spurs with decorated leather straps, iron shanks with silver mountings. Rowels have rounded prongs*

Saddles & Stirrups

2775

Over the centuries the saddle evolved from a simple invention designed to facilitate remaining on a horse to a highly specialized tool in a major industry. By the time the conquistadores moved into America, saddlery itself had acquired the status of a folk art that was often carried to extraordinary extremes. A Spanish *caballero* was a gentleman, and he would not consider outfitting his horse with unadorned gear.

The most painstaking attention was focused on the construction and leatherwork of the Andalusian saddle, a distinctly functional form that was enhanced by the expert hand-tooling and stitching that had long been Spain's special pride. The wooden framework of the saddle, known as the tree, was wrapped with rawhide to prevent splitting. Stirrups were attached directly to the tree, and the frame was then covered with leather. The saddle had a high pommel—a most important part, as it

2776

2777

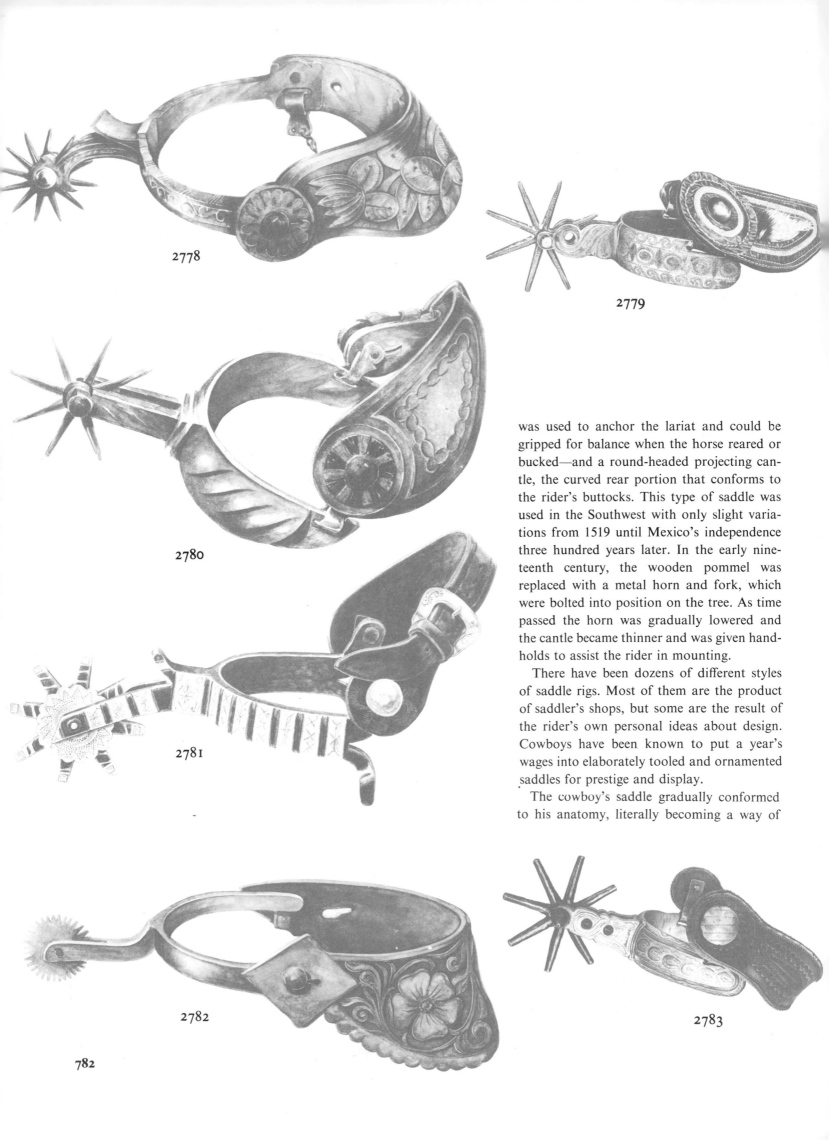

2778

2779

2780

2781

782

2782

2783

was used to anchor the lariat and could be gripped for balance when the horse reared or bucked—and a round-headed projecting cantle, the curved rear portion that conforms to the rider's buttocks. This type of saddle was used in the Southwest with only slight variations from 1519 until Mexico's independence three hundred years later. In the early nineteenth century, the wooden pommel was replaced with a metal horn and fork, which were bolted into position on the tree. As time passed the horn was gradually lowered and the cantle became thinner and was given handholds to assist the rider in mounting.

There have been dozens of different styles of saddle rigs. Most of them are the product of saddler's shops, but some are the result of the rider's own personal ideas about design. Cowboys have been known to put a year's wages into elaborately tooled and ornamented saddles for prestige and display.

The cowboy's saddle gradually conformed to his anatomy, literally becoming a way of

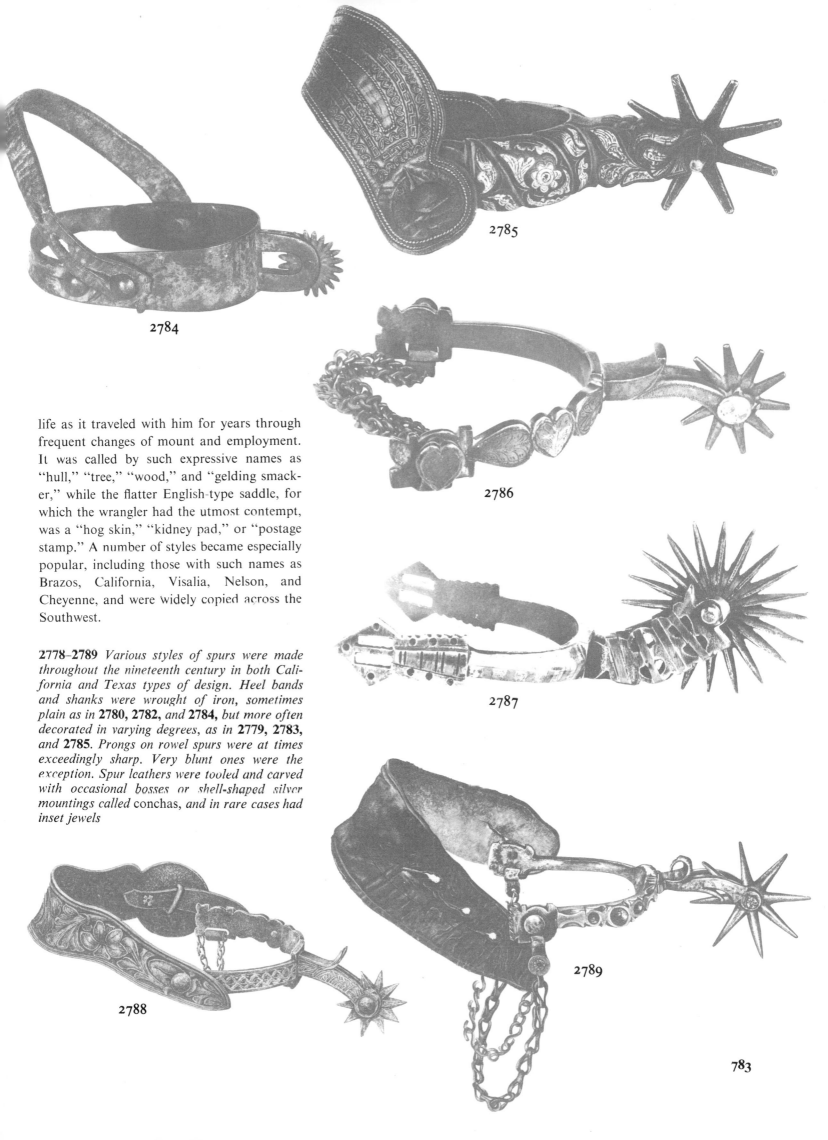

2784

2785

2786

2787

life as it traveled with him for years through frequent changes of mount and employment. It was called by such expressive names as "hull," "tree," "wood," and "gelding smacker," while the flatter English-type saddle, for which the wrangler had the utmost contempt, was a "hog skin," "kidney pad," or "postage stamp." A number of styles became especially popular, including those with such names as Brazos, California, Visalia, Nelson, and Cheyenne, and were widely copied across the Southwest.

2778–2789 Various styles of spurs were made throughout the nineteenth century in both California and Texas types of design. Heel bands and shanks were wrought of iron, sometimes plain as in 2780, 2782, and 2784, but more often decorated in varying degrees, as in 2779, 2783, and 2785. Prongs on rowel spurs were at times exceedingly sharp. Very blunt ones were the exception. Spur leathers were tooled and carved with occasional bosses or shell-shaped silver mountings called conchas, *and in rare cases had inset jewels*

2788

2789

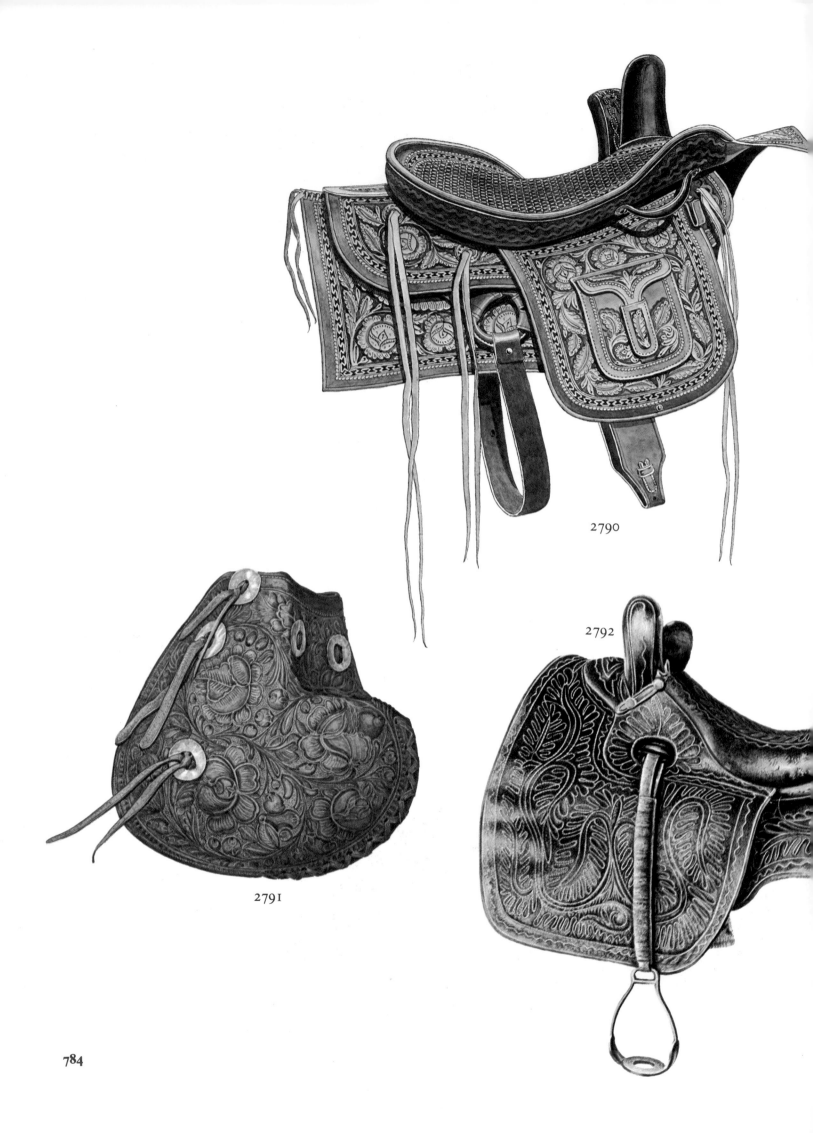

2790

2791

2792

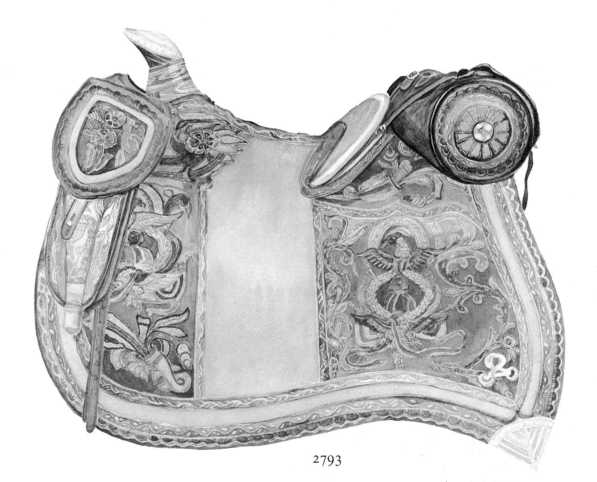

2793

2794

2790 Sidesaddle of richly carved leather with low cantled seat, extra pouch on side flap, leather tie strings. A product of the 1880s 2791 Full leather stirrup decorated and tooled with roses, petals, and foliage patterns 2792 Lady's sidesaddle from California. Rich all-over decorative effect produced entirely by skillful stitching of palmettes and meanders 2793 Officer's saddle with roll pouch behind low cantled seat and pistol holster at pommel. Decorated with American symbols including eagles and head of George Washington, c. 1860–65 2794 The fine art of the saddlemaker is shown in the delicate tooling of naturalistic roses and rosebuds in this child's saddle, c. 1860

2795 *Saddle bag with leaf forms and border of stamped units. Made in San Francisco, late nineteenth century* **2796** *Heavily ornamented California saddle with lavish use of silver conchas, sprigs of roses, lions, and corner units on upper and lower skirts, cantle, pommel, side jockey, stirrup, and fender. Dated 1888. Photograph* **2797** *California-style saddle with graceful swirling leaf forms on skirts, side jockey, sudadero or fender, and tapadero covering the stirrup* **2798** *Left side of child's saddle shown in* **2774**. *Velvet-upholstered seat is quilted and embroidered. Made in Monterey, California, c. 1820* **2799** *California saddle hand-tooled with a floral and leaf motif consistently used on every part. Made in 1855. Photograph* **2800** *Full leather stirrup with chased-silver boss. Photograph* **2801** *Extensive tooling of naturalistic decoration well designed to conform to leather areas in skirts, fork covering, side jockey, and stirrup strap. Cinch band of woven wool has full leathered rings* **2802** *Child's saddle of tan cowhide. Made in San Angelo, Texas, 1844*

2799

2800

2801

2802

787

The Squire of Mount Vernon

2804

N<small>O OTHER AMERICAN</small> hero has been as much revered or variously represented as George Washington. Our first president seems to have been a willing and gracious sitter in spite of his busy schedule, for during his lifetime some twenty-seven different artists painted or sculpted his likeness. Gilbert Stuart alone did about one hundred portraits of Washington. Charles Willson Peale and members of his illustrious family pursued their idol with great tenacity, and on one occasion all joined in at once to sketch the president from every angle. France's noted

2803 General Washington on *a* White Charger, *painted by an unknown artist in New York, c.1830. National Gallery of Art, Washington, D.C. Gift of Edgar William and Bernice Chrysler Garbisch*
2804 *Carved oval plaque of George Washington by Samuel McIntire*
2805 *View of the river front of the mansion at Mount Vernon as it originally looked. The modest dwelling was remodeled and enlarged several times, beginning in 1757. Photograph courtesy Mount Vernon Ladies' Association, Mount Vernon, Virginia*

2805

3

sculptor Jean Antoine Houdon was sent by his government in 1785 to produce the familiar bust that has served as the model for a great many stamps and coins. When Washington visited Salem, Massachusetts, in 1789, the famed architectural woodcarver Samuel McIntire sketched him as he addressed the townspeople from the courthouse balcony. From this informal model the artist was able to carve an excellent oval plaque that measured approximately three feet by five.

It is only natural that the man who led the Revolutionary forces with such skill and courage should have become a legend in his own day. During the trying times of his administration and through the years of retirement this reverence continued to gain in intensity and the citizenry came to endow him with godlike qualities. Manifestations of this adoration are to be found in any survey of the handicrafts of the time. In the backwoods of New England, Vermont housewives devoted long evenings to hooking "Father of Our Country" rugs, while in the southern Highlands Carolina carpenters whittled busts out of pine planks.

Upon Washington's death in December, 1799, this reverence assumed renewed vigor, and he became a symbol of national unity and patriotism. Engravings, cotton goods, medals, bills and coins, and a great variety of memorabilia were produced. Craftsmen and folk artists alike were spurred to a feverish pitch of activity, perpetuating Washington's image in statues, busts, andirons, porcelain and pottery, quilts and coverlets, cretonnes, and wallpaper patterns. When pressed glass became popular, Washington's likeness appeared on bowls, dishes, and flasks, and the development of Currier and Ives' famous prints eventually made it possible for even the poorest family to display his likeness.

To catalogue the ways in which the first president's face and figure have appeared over the years would require an encyclopedic study. Unlike the American eagle, whose popularity varies with the mood of the country, the Washington mystique remains unchallenged and unwavering, as solid as Plymouth Rock.

2806 *In 1823 Rembrandt Peale painted a portrait of Washington which became known as the "porthole" portrait because of its circular frame. This mid-nineteenth-century mezzotint showing the full bust surrounded by an oak wreath, the whole engraved to represent a sculpture in stone, was done by Adam B. Walter, after the Peale painting. Courtesy New York Public Library, New York City*

PATRIÆ PATER

791

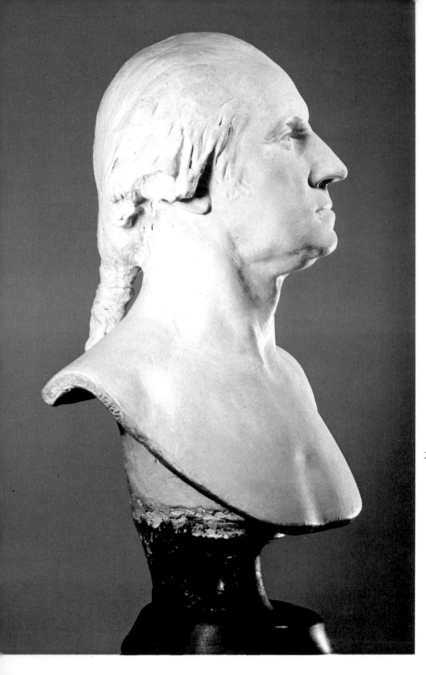

2807

2808

2807 *Bust of Washington by Jean Antoine Houdon, executed during his visit to Mount Vernon in 1785. Photograph courtesy Mount Vernon Ladies' Association, Mount Vernon, Virginia* **2808** *Cotton-printed textile featuring Washington and the newly elected president Benjamin Harrison, 1889* **2809** *Printed textile showing profile of Washington in a wreath of flowers*

2809

2810

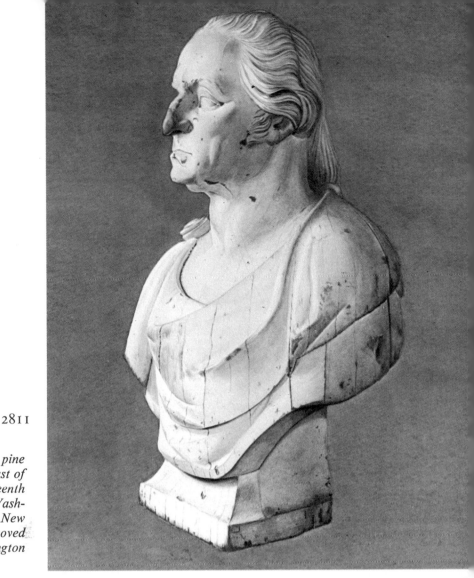

2811

2810 *This equestrian figure, carved in low relief on a pine plank, is the work of a native craftsman, 1902* 2811 *Bust of Washington carved in pine and painted white. Late nineteenth century* 2812 *Polychromed wooden statue of General Washington carved in 1776. It was erected in Bowling Green, New York, after the statue of King George had been removed* 2813 *Printed textiles showing portraits of George Washington were issued throughout the nineteenth century*

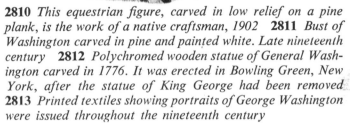

2812

2813

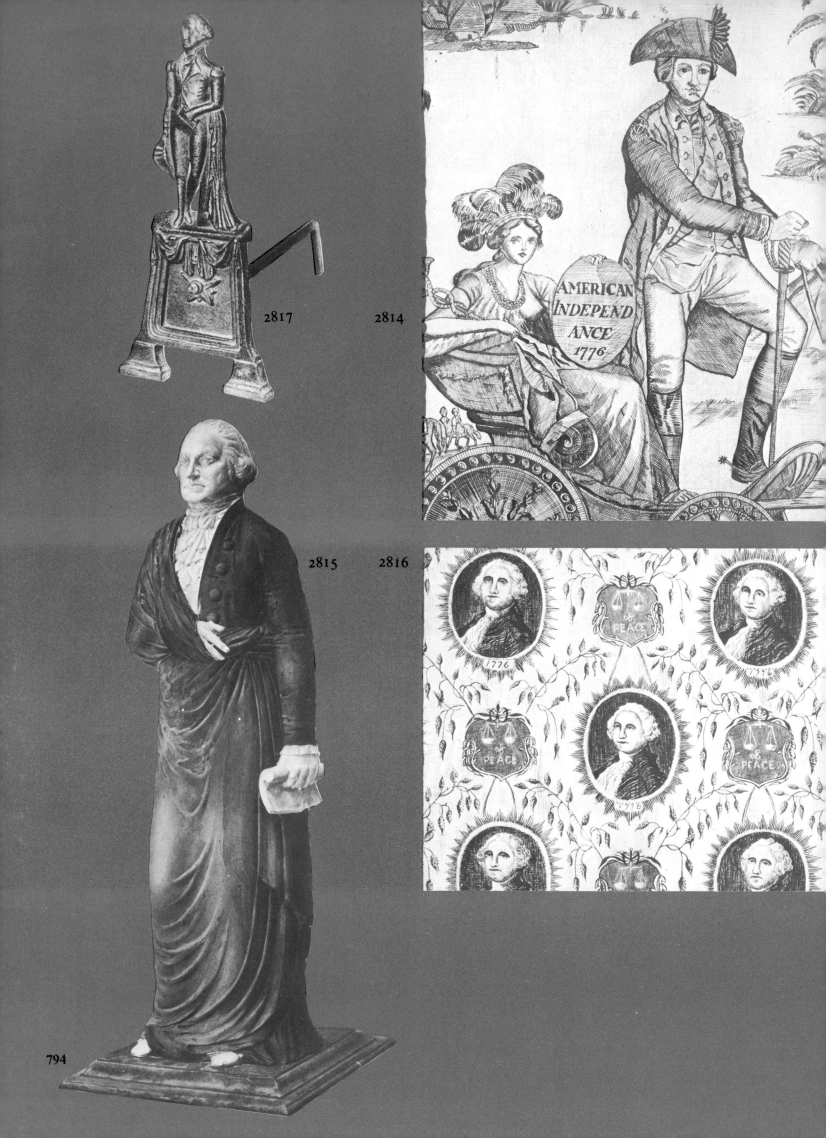

2817

2814

2815

2816

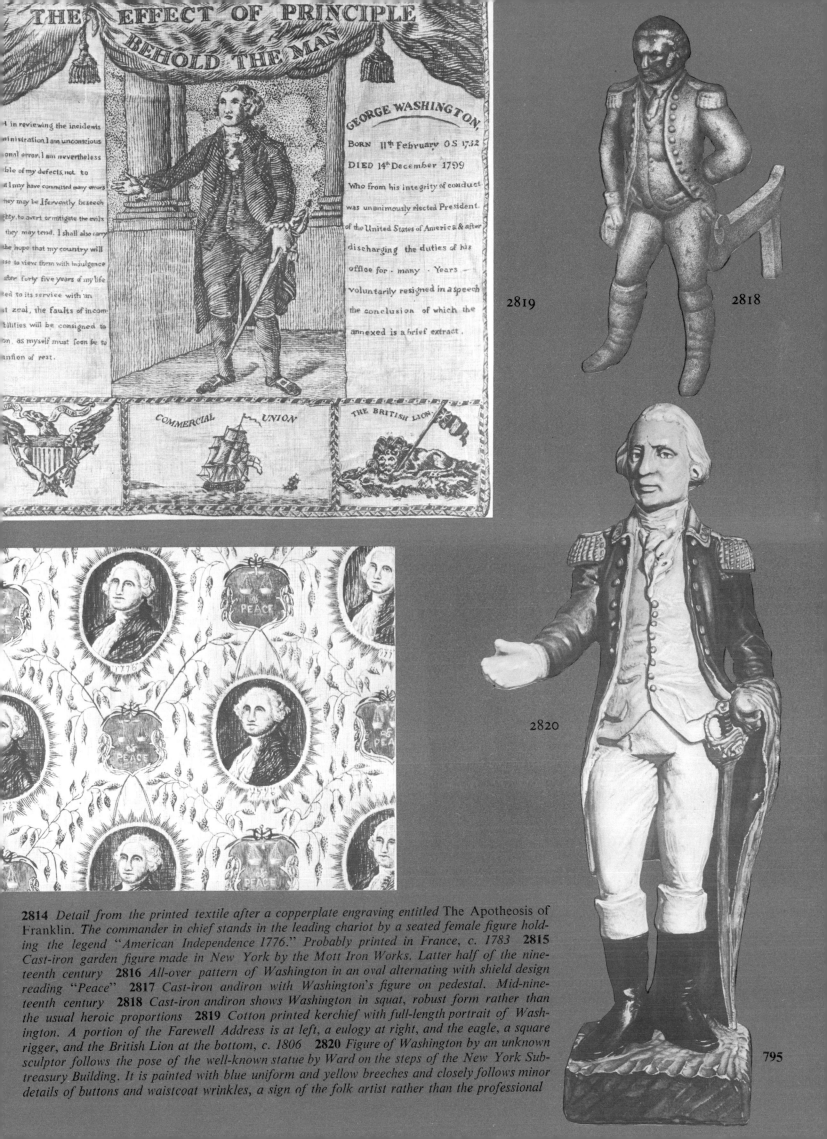

THE EFFECT OF PRINCIPLE

BEHOLD THE MAN

...t in reviewing the incidents
...ministration I am unconscious
...onal error, I am nevertheless
...ible of my defects, not to
...t I may have committed many errors
...hey may be I fervently beseech
...ghty, to avert or mitigate the evils
...they may tend, I shall also carry
...he hope that my country will
...ase to view them with indulgence
...after forty five years of my life
...ted to its service with an
...t zeal, the faults of incom-
...bilities will be consigned to
...on, as myself must soon be to
...ansion of rest.

GEORGE WASHINGTON,
Born 11th February O S 1732
Died 14th December 1799
Who from his integrity of conduct
was unanimously elected President
of the United States of America & after
discharging the duties of his
office for many Years
voluntarily resigned in a speech
the conclusion of which the
annexed is a brief extract.

COMMERCIAL UNION

THE BRITISH LION

2819

2818

2820

795

2814 *Detail from the printed textile after a copperplate engraving entitled* The Apotheosis of Franklin. *The commander in chief stands in the leading chariot by a seated female figure hold-ing the legend "American Independence 1776." Probably printed in France, c. 1783* **2815** *Cast-iron garden figure made in New York by the Mott Iron Works. Latter half of the nine-teenth century* **2816** *All-over pattern of Washington in an oval alternating with shield design reading "Peace"* **2817** *Cast-iron andiron with Washington's figure on pedestal. Mid-nine-teenth century* **2818** *Cast-iron andiron shows Washington in squat, robust form rather than the usual heroic proportions* **2819** *Cotton printed kerchief with full-length portrait of Wash-ington. A portion of the Farewell Address is at left, a eulogy at right, and the eagle, a square rigger, and the British Lion at the bottom, c. 1806* **2820** *Figure of Washington by an unknown sculptor follows the pose of the well-known statue by Ward on the steps of the New York Sub-treasury Building. It is painted with blue uniform and yellow breeches and closely follows minor details of buttons and waistcoat wrinkles, a sign of the folk artist rather than the professional*

2821

2821 *Three-foot high seated figure of Liberty, by Eliodoro Patete of West Virginia. The artist's familiarity with Italian religious art is revealed in the academic attitude of the figure, which suggests a Madonna. The books, stars, diadem, and especially the inscriptions are all characteristic of folk-art expression, c. 1865* **2822,** *Cast-iron Liberty Bell coin banks produced at the time of the great Philadelphia Centennial in 1876* **2823** *Statue of Liberty coin bank, a type very popular following the statue's unveiling in New York harbor in 1886*

2822

Symbols of Freedom

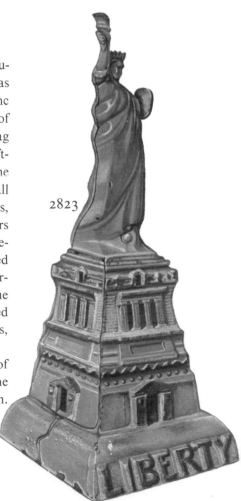

2823

BEFORE THE AMERICAN colonies became independent, on festive occasions, when custom called for a display of colors, the Union Jack was unfurled and images of Britannia were in evidence. With the Revolutionary War and the Declaration of Independence, these symbols of English domination were, of course, abandoned: the new republic required its own official emblems, a flag and a state seal.

On June, 14, 1777, Congress adopted a new flag, but various flags were used during the Revolutionary War. For example, beneath a banner of crimson and silver with the legend "Conquer or Die!" the embattled farmers at Concord Bridge fired "the shot heard round the world"; beneath the Pine Tree banner the battle of Bunker Hill was lost and won; and beneath the Rattlesnake flag the American fleet won its first victory. Hence, to sever the last link that bound the Colonies individually to England, the Stars and Stripes was created as a symbol of national unity. The thirteen red and white stripes, one for each of the states, had been a feature of an earlier flag that included the Union Jack in the upper left-hand quadrant, but the resolution on the design for the new flag replaced the small Union Jack motif with thirteen white stars, symbolizing a new constellation. (These stars were usually arranged in a circle, but placement varied.) It was this flag that represented the new country when Lord Cornwallis surrendered in 1781, and it had already become such an accepted symbol that it was displayed widely and figured importantly in paintings, carvings, needlecraft, and metalwork.

While the flag was adopted within a year of Independence Day, the Great Seal with the American eagle required longer deliberation.

At the beginning of the Revolution, Congress appointed a committee of prominent citizens —among them George Washington, Benjamin Franklin, Thomas Jefferson, and John Adams —whose task it was to devise and design a seal, or official coat of arms, that would incorporate the ideals, aspirations, and unity of the young republic. They met on the afternoon of July 4, 1776, a few hours after the signing of the Declaration of Independence. Some of the designs discussed for the seal were quite fantastic; for example, Thomas Jefferson suggested a seal that would depict the Israelites crossing the Red Sea and the Pharoah's army being destroyed. Six years elapsed while committees met and disbanded, and one design after another was proposed and rejected. In May, 1782, a third committee submitted to Congress a design by William Barton, an authority on heraldry. Barton's design incorporated an eagle—"the Symbol of Supreme Power and Authority, signifying the Congress." The Continental Congress did not consider this design acceptable either, however, and Charles Thompson, secretary of that body, took over. Thompson eliminated the allegorical figures which had appeared on previous designs and made the eagle—specifically the American bald eagle—the central motif, "holding in his dexter talon an olive branch [symbolizing peace] and in his sinister a bundle of arrows [representing war]." (Barton's eagle had held a sword and a flag.) Over the eagle's head was a constellation of thirteen stars and in its beak a scroll bearing the motto *E Pluribus Unum*. This motto was the one feature surviving from the design submitted by the first committee. The verso side showed a pyramid symbolizing stability and permanence with the Eye of Providence at its top. After some additional changes by Barton—he supplied thirteen alternating white and red vertical stripes below the rectangular blue field on the eagle's breast—the seal was adopted by the then revolting Colonies on June 20, 1782. It was later approved by the Philadelphia Federal

Constitutional Convention of 1787, and was in common use by the time of George Washington's inauguration in 1789.

To date, there have been seven dies of the Great Seal. The fourth and fifth dies, cast in 1841 and 1847, were criticized because the eagle's left talon did not hold the thirteen arrows specified in the original legislation passed by Congress. In 1884, at the request of Theodore Frelinghuysen, secretary of state, Congress appropriated a thousand dollars for the preparation of a new die. A new seal showing the correct number of arrows was made the following year by James Horton Whitehouse, chief designer for Tiffany and Company. His design is the one in use today.

The Stars and Stripes, along with the Great Seal and the American eagle, provided artists, designers, and craftsmen with emblems that have been used for almost two centuries. The eagle, whose use as a symbol descended from antiquity, proved a particularly versatile decorative motif. Without studying, much less submitting to, the artistic conventions governing heraldry, American artists and craftsmen intuitively recognized that there were few limits to the decorative potential of the newly adopted national symbol. Thus a profusion of decorative eagles appeared from the time of the War of 1812 through the Civil War.

Other popular patriotic emblems included the figures of Columbia and Uncle Sam—the former a poetic, the latter a comic, symbol of the United States—and of Liberty, the Liberty Bell, Independence Hall, and likenesses of George Washington.

During the closing years of the eighteenth century and the first decades of the nineteenth, artists and craftsmen used these national symbols to express the period's patriotic fervor. In the works of folk artists these motifs were given a fresh and earthy vitality. More, perhaps, than in any other period of American history, such folk works seem to spring directly from the heart and thus are exceptionally effective expressions of the ideals of freedom and unity.

2824

2825

2826

2827

2828

2829

2830

2824 *Carved eagle in which natural proportions have been sacrificed to emphasize head, beak, and talons* **2825** *Sheet-brass powder horn displaying elaborate military motif. Late eighteenth century* **2826** *Painted cast-iron mirror frame topped by an eagle. Patriotic motifs include flags, shield, officer in medallion, 1862* **2827** *Carved and painted pine sea chest, combining maritime symbols— anchor and fisherman's head—with patriotic motif of eagle and shield. Made in Massachusetts, c. 1840* **2828** *Stamped sheet-brass eagle, used as decoration on parade floats and platforms, 1840–50* **2829** *Columbia weather vane with thirty-two-star flag. Made of cast zinc, sheet copper, and brass, c. 1865* **2830** *Painted eagle appears on many regimental drums of Civil War vintage*

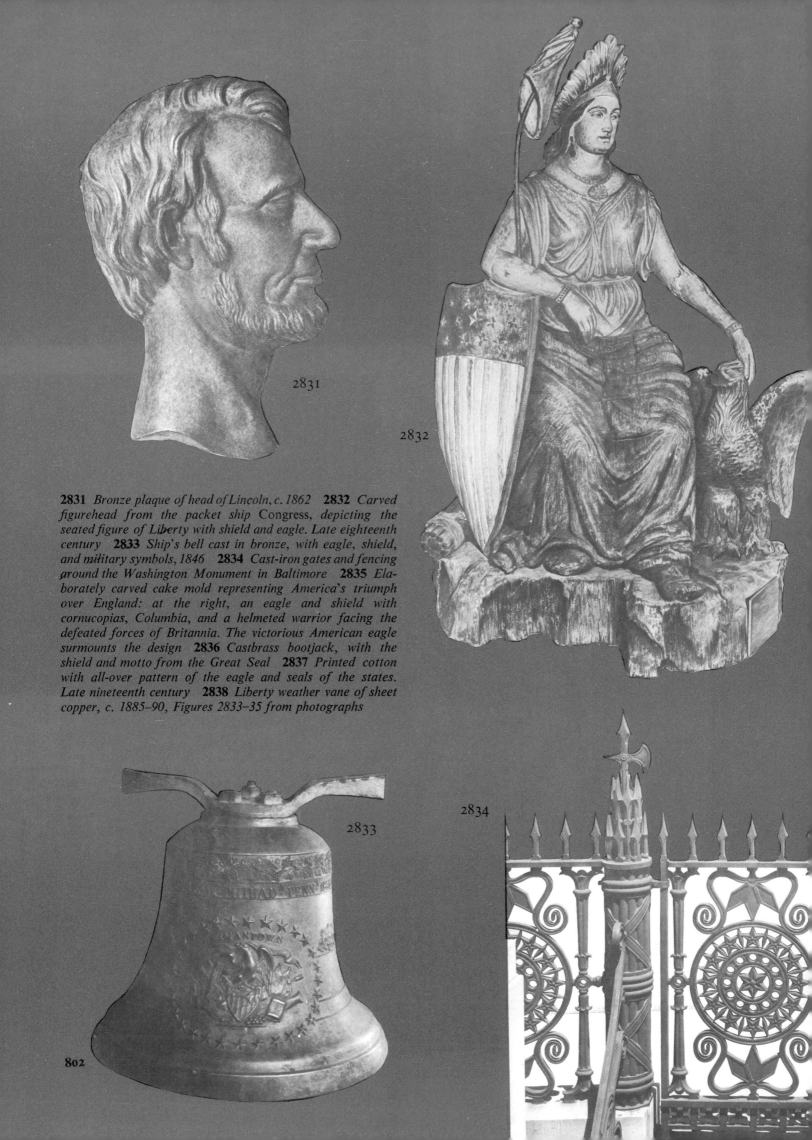

2831 Bronze plaque of head of Lincoln, c. 1862 **2832** Carved figurehead from the packet ship Congress, depicting the seated figure of Liberty with shield and eagle. Late eighteenth century **2833** Ship's bell cast in bronze, with eagle, shield, and military symbols, 1846 **2834** Cast-iron gates and fencing around the Washington Monument in Baltimore **2835** Elaborately carved cake mold representing America's triumph over England: at the right, an eagle and shield with cornucopias, Columbia, and a helmeted warrior facing the defeated forces of Britannia. The victorious American eagle surmounts the design **2836** Castbrass bootjack, with the shield and motto from the Great Seal **2837** Printed cotton with all-over pattern of the eagle and seals of the states. Late nineteenth century **2838** Liberty weather vane of sheet copper, c. 1885–90, Figures 2833–35 from photographs

2835

2836

2837

2838

803

2840

The Eagle Spreads Its Wings

THE EAGLE HAS long been the most popular American motif in the decorative arts and crafts. Thousands of artists and craftsmen have interpreted its image. Soaring and circling far above the earth, plunging like a meteor from the sky, screaming defiance at a storm, or fiercely striking its prey—to men of every age the eagle has embodied freedom and power. This image has been emblazoned on the chariots of warriors and on the shields of knights from the time of Caesar to the battle of Iwo Jima.

A bald-headed eagle of the American species with outspread wings and legs is prominently displayed on the Great Seal of the United States, which was approved by Congress on June 20, 1782. The use of the bird followed ancient precedents. Three thousand years before Christ the eagle had been guardian deity of Mesopotamia and had also represented Babylonia, depicted in a pose similar to that on the Great Seal.

In ancient Greece and its colonial states, the eagle, holding a thunderbolt or its prey, was for long a favorite emblem on coins. It also appeared on Roman coins, medals, and gems, often with a palm branch in its talons. The standard of the Roman legions was a spread eagle, encircled by a laurel wreath and grasp-

2839 *Eagle signboard with the owner's name, J. Procter, hung outside the entrance to the Red Lion Inn at Red Lion, Delaware. Washington is known to have stopped here, for an entry in his diary for March 1791 notes that he gave his horses "a bite of Hay at the Red Lyon" on his way to Mount Vernon. Photograph courtesy the Henry Francis du Pont Winterthur Museum, Winterthur, Delaware* **2840** *Painted pine eagle clutching arrows and shield. Carved by Samuel McIntire in 1805. From the customhouse at Salem* **2841** *Pine sternboard eagle with foliated scrolls or rinceaux. Early nineteenth century*

2841

ing a thunderbolt in both talons. During the Middle Ages, eagles with either single or double heads flourished as heraldic devices. Thus the selection of the eagle as a national emblem was influenced by medieval and Classical models, the latter of which were simultaneously very influential in other areas of art, notably architecture.

The eagle on the Great Seal was by no means the first emblematic eagle to make its appearance in the American Colonies. As early as 1700, one was stamped on a New York token of lead or brass; in 1776 it was featured on a Massachusetts copper penny within a semicircle of thirteen stars; and in 1778 the State of New York included an eagle perched on a globe as part of its official coat of arms. However, the eagle of the Great Seal is the first specified as being of the American bald-headed species, "bald" in the older sense of the term, meaning white.

A bald-headed American eagle was also incorporated in a design by Major l'Enfant for a badge for the Society of Cincinnati, a group founded in 1783 by members of the American revolutionary army. Benjamin Franklin, although well-informed in a wide variety of fields, was apparently no ornithologist, and on seeing the badge, he wrote to his daughter from France: "I am, on this account, not displeased that the figure is not known as a bald eagle but looks more like a turkey. For in truth, the turkey is in comparison a much more respectable bird and withal a true original native of America. Eagles have been found in all countries, but the turkey is peculiar to ours. . . . He is, besides, (though a little vain and silly, it is true, but not the worse emblem for that) a bird of courage, and would not hesitate to attack a grenadier of the British guards, who should presume to invade his farmyard with a red coat on." In the preceding paragraph Franklin had expressed the wish that "the bald eagle had not been chosen

as the representative of our country; he is a bird of bad moral character; he does not get his living honestly . . . too lazy to fish for himself, he watches the labor of the fishing-hawk, and when that diligent bird has at length taken a fish, and is bearing it to his nest for the support of his mate and his young ones, the bald eagle pursues him and takes it from him . . . like those men who live by sharping and robbing he is generally poor, and often very lousy. Besides he is a rank coward; the little king-bird, not bigger than a sparrow, attacks him boldly and drives him out of the district."

In *The American Eagle, A Study in Natural and Civil History*, Francis Hobart Herrick comes stoutly to the defense of the national bird, clearing him of Franklin's charges. Herrick suggests that the accusations may have been inspired by pique, since Franklin's own design for the seal—he had been chairman of the first committee—had been rejected. Herrick describes the bald eagle as a native who has never been known to leave the continent of his own volition, who nests as near the sun as he can get, "like a true bird of Jove and messenger of the star of the day," and as a model parent, devoting six months or more to rearing his young. "He does not live entirely or mainly by 'robbing' or 'sharping,' as Benjamin Franklin seemed to believe, but is an expert fisherman in his own right, and he will not rob the osprey unless this bird is heedless in giving him the chance, or, as it were, offers him the challenge . . . above all the eagle is no rank coward, as Franklin also mistakenly supposed. Contrary to that savant's opinion, he is never driven from the neighborhood by the little kingbird, or by any other living being except-ing a man armed with a gun. . . . Woe to any impudent marauder who assails the castle of the king of the air when eggs and eaglets are in danger. . . . The truth of the matter is that the eagle has learned from bitter experience that he is king of birds only, and that where man

2842 2843

808

2844 2845

2846

2847

2848

2842 *Carved pine eagle, probably made in Newport, Rhode Island, c. 1830* **2843** *Ribbed whisky flask with eagle in oval. Made by Louisville, Kentucky, glassworks* **2844** *Cast-brass eagle, mounted on an acorn-shaped walnut base* **2845** *Pine eagle, nearly five feet tall, said to have served as a signboard for an unidentified "Eagle Tavern" in Rhode Island. Feathers on breast, wings, and back, individually cut in high relief, reveal powerful carving, c. 1850–75. Photograph courtesy Colonial Williamsburg* **2846** *Ceramic eagle used as a mantel decoration* **2847** *Snare drum of bent-wood with painted eagle, mid-nineteenth century* **2848** *Coverlet with woven design including eagle, the most popular motif in the first half of the nineteenth century*

2849

enters the picture, caution and circumspection are the price of life, liberty and independence." Herrick adds that if the eagle had possessed the brains of the dodo, he would have been virtually extinct by the end of the eighteenth century.

After the adoption of the Great Seal, a variety of eagles appeared on other seals and insignia, including those for departments of the federal and state governments and the presidential seal, and on coins. Frequently, as on the presidential seal, the eagle turns its head to the left, whereas on the Great Seal the head turns toward the right, which is considered the correct position. Other variations include placing arrows in the right claw and the olive branch in the left, reducing the number of arrows or of stripes in the shield, and placing the eagle on the shield instead of the shield on the eagle. Some people condemn these revisions for not conforming to heraldic law. Various eagles, especially those on coins, have also been criticized for being of alien breed, for example, for having the long feathered trousers characteristic of the golden eagle; whereas the American eagle, except in its juvenal stage, has

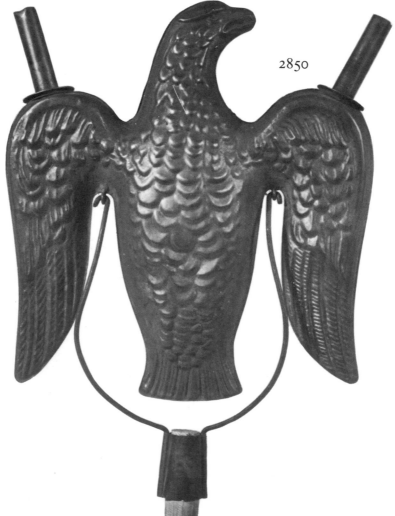

2850

bare or half-bare shanks, extremely conspicuous because they are bright yellow.

At Washington's inauguration, the eagle's popularity increased. After taking office, Washington made a triumphal tour of the thirteen states and was greeted everywhere with eagle transparencies traced on starched and whitewashed windowpanes, behind which blazing candles produced dramatic effects. At balls in the President's honor, fans and ribbons displayed painted eagles, and men's lapels carried engraved ones in brass. Washington himself had become a confirmed eagle lover; a spread eagle was perched on the finial of his desk at Mount Vernon, and an eagle was carved above his pew in St. Paul's Church. Within a few years, the eagle had become the country's most popular decorative motif. The War of 1812 produced another patriotic upsurge, fanned by the fervor of renewed activities against Britain, that expressed itself in the arts and crafts. After the war, craftsmen worked the bird of freedom into an extraordinary number and variety of designs. Subsequent nineteenth-century presidential campaigns, patriotic celebrations, and national

2852

2853

2849 *Cast-iron eagle, nineteenth century* **2850** *Soldered sheet-brass eagle torch, used in the Mexican War, 1848* **2851** *Cast-iron eagle pin tray, c. 1870–80* **2852** *Brass eagle door knocker, c. 1850* **2853** *Brass eagle door knocker, c. 1840–50*

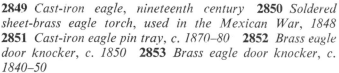

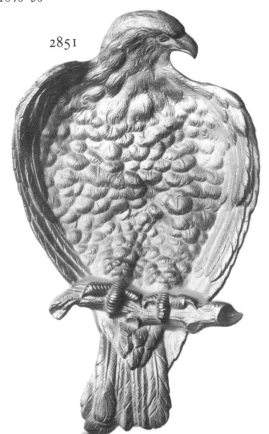

2851

811

2854

2855

2856

2857

2854 *Eagle weather vane, nineteenth century. Photograph courtesy the Smithsonian Institution, Washington, D.C.* 2855 *Gilded wood eagle and snake, nineteenth century* 2856 *Carved eagle with shield and arrows. Photograph courtesy the Smithsonian Institution, Washington, D.C.* 2857 *Cast-iron eagle flagpole holder, 1856* 2858 *Carved eagle ornament. Photograph courtesy the Smithsonian Institution, Washington, D.C.* 2859 *Carved eagle figurehead, early nineteenth century* 2860 *Cast-iron eagle desk ornament* 2861 *Eagle with realistically detailed feathers and proportions revealing a strong Napoleonic influence, especially in the bolts of lightning clutched by the talons*

2858

2859

2860

2861

2862

2863

2864

emergencies brought forth new crops of eagles.

With appropriate democratic impartiality, the eagle lent itself to the decoration of porcelain dinner services—which were imported from England and China because an American porcelain industry was slow to develop but which used American motifs—and kitchen crockery. It was impressed into whisky flasks and Sandwich glass, woven into curtain and upholstery fabrics, and perched as a finial on mirrors, clocks, and weather vanes. It was carved into butter stamps and delicately inlaid in drawing-room furniture, painted on tavern signs and cast into flatiron holders, and even stitched in quilted counterpanes, complete with arrows, olive branch, scroll, and overhead stars. The eagle was also minted in a number of forms, but its image on coins and paper

2865

money is not nearly as varied as are its manifestations on other types of objects.

Throughout the nineteenth century, the
eagle was a favorite motif for stoneware.
Early examples were small and crisply incised;
the later ones were large, brushed on in cobalt
blue with bold calligraphic strokes, or molded
in relief. Pennsylvania German potters some-

2866

2862 *Cast-iron eagle standing on cloud formation. Made by the Meeker Foundry in Newark,
New Jersey, c. 1850* **2863** *Cast-iron stove urn
with eagle finial, c. 1850. Photograph* **2864**
*Wooden eagle, carved in low relief as marine
decoration* **2865** *Gilded copper eagle ornament,
nineteenth century*

2866 *Powder flask with eagle, crossed pistols,
and motto* E Pluribus Unum. *Made in 1778.*
2867 *Cast-iron eagle ornament. Photograph*

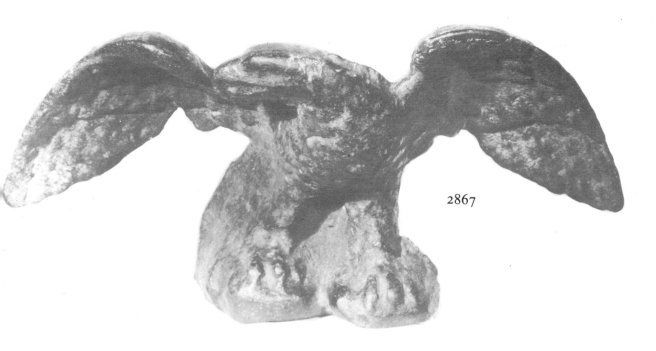

2867

2868

2869

2870

2871

2872

2873

2874

2875

2868–2875 *Eagles were usually carved from pine, which is easily cut and gouged. Those of wide wingspread generally necessitated carving the wings as separate pieces, which were then supported and strengthened with metal cleats (**2869** and **2875**.) More static poses, as in **2872** and **2873**, were used on flagpoles or weather vanes. Nineteenth century*

2876

2877

times incised the eagle in pie plates, in celebration of presidential candidates. Handsomely stylized eagles appeared on wooden butter stamps of Pennsylvania German origin. These were carved by folk artists, usually in intaglio so that the design impressed on the butter would appear in relief.

Spirited and beautiful eagles were introduced in pieced, knotted, and other types of quilts which exhibit skilled craftsmanship and the creativity of many generations of American women. Weavers were not content simply to make the eagle the central motif of the coverlet, but worked the bird into elaborate borders in repeat patterns. Commemorative textiles featured the eagle and told the nation's story through pictorial scenes and symbolic motifs. Some of these celebrated the Mexican War,

2878

2879

others commemorated the Philadelphia Centennial, and still others were issued at the time of Benjamin Harrison's inauguration in 1889, which was also the centenary of Washington's election and the year in which the state of Washington was admitted to the Union.

The most interesting and beautiful eagles are found among those carved in wood, either in relief or in the round, as decorative panels for sofas, chairs, and mantelpieces; over the doorways of public buildings or private dwellings; on cupolas and gateposts; as shop or tavern signs; or as figureheads. This medium—mahogany and pine were the preferred woods—attracted both self-taught folk artists and trained sculptors, architects, and cabinetmakers. Fine marquetry eagles were inlaid in mahogany, satinwood, and maple

2880

2876 *Carved wooden eagle, attributed to Samuel McIntire, c. 1800. Photograph.* **2877** *Copper eagle weather vane, mid-nineteenth century* **2878** *Colored and gilded eagle, carved from mahogany, c. 1800–1810, by the noted sculptor William Rush. In Independence Hall, Philadelphia. Photograph* **2879** *Eagle figurehead with eighteen-foot wingspread. Carved by John Haley Bellamy for the U.S.S.* Lancaster, *c. 1880–90* **2880** *Eagle and banner, carved in low relief. Conventional style of execution with a minimum of incised strokes. Made by John Haley Bellamy* **2881** *Carved eagle, gilded and polychromed. Feather treatment approaches acanthus foliation*

2881

2882

chests, slant-top and tambour desks, secretaries, tall clocks, knife boxes, and tilt-top tables. The number of inlaid stars in a piece was usually the same as the number of states in the Union at the time, which helps to date the piece.

First among the untrained craftsmen was the Pennsylvania German whittler Wilhelm Schimmel, who worked during the post-Civil War years. Of the academicians, one of the most distinguished was America's first native-born sculptor, William Rush (1756–1833), among whose surviving works are two magnificent eagles carved as emblems, one for a church and the other for a fire company. Samuel McIntire, born a year after Rush, has been called the most celebrated of the craftsmen-architects of America. He was fond of making an eagle in relief against a background of stars the central motif of his exquisite mantelpieces, and of cresting the rails of his equally beautiful mahogany sofas with the emblem. He also executed eagles in the round

with closed wings and eagles perched on globes as ornaments for gate arches and cupolas. Among his works is a noble spread eagle which was placed over the door of the Old Custom House in his native Salem. McIntire's New York contemporary, Duncan Phyfe, like other cabinetmakers of the period, made charming mahogany chairs with eagle splats for distinguished clients.

Another outstanding artist-craftsman of a more recent period was John Haley Bellamy (1836–1914) of Kittery Point, Maine. He devoted most of his life to carving eagles, finding his chief employment with the Boston and Portsmouth navy yards and the government. He made ornamental eagles for public and private buildings and innumerable small spread eagles, many of which were brilliantly painted and gilded and were placed over the doorways of ships' cabins. He developed a special technique for stylizing his eagles, which are extremely graceful and proud, with fierce beaks, usually holding a banner carrying

2883

2884

a patriotic motto. Possibly his most ambitious one is the huge figurehead for the U.S.S. *Lancaster,* carved in 1859. This gigantic bird has a wingspread of more than eighteen feet and weighs about thirty-two hundred pounds.

Cast-iron eagles are probably as numerous and diverse in character as those carved in wood. They range from such small objects as a delicately molded pin tray and a mechanical bank in the form of an eagle feeding its young to a majestic creature with a wingspread of sixty-five inches, once used as a sign. Sometimes these eagles appear to derive from European prototypes and to have been adapted by tradition-loving craftsmen to new patriotic uses. In addition to gold, silver, and bronze coins and medallions which featured the image of the eagle, sheet copper was hammered into eagle weather vanes. In early Pennsylvania food "safes," the tinplate ventilating holes were sometimes pricked in eagle patterns. Furniture mounts, and particularly the finials of clocks, featured many types of brass eagles.

In retrospect, it seems fortunate that the founding fathers chose the eagle, which could be easily rendered and interpreted in most mediums in a great variety of attitudes—perching, preening, soaring, gliding, attacking, and alighting. For the versatility of our national symbol has continued to inspire countless artists and artisans.

2882–2885 *The spread eagle took many forms, with and without accessory decorations, as a motif ideally suited to the stern of a ship. The horizontal extension of the wings varied from five to eight feet. In contrast to the figurehead at the bow, which called for treatment in the round, sternboard eagles were executed in comparatively low relief. Coupled with the eagle were such design elements as flags, drapes, the shield, and the ribbon bearing the motto* E Pluribus Unum. *A fine example of gilded pine carved by Alton Skillin for the U.S.S.* Enterprise *in 1881 is shown in 2882. The eagle and shield in 2883 were carved by John Bellamy*

2885

2886

2887 2888

822

2886 *Painted pine eagle, by William Rush, c. 1810. Photograph courtesy Philadelphia Museum of Art* **2887** *Glass plate, with eagle clutching arrows and olive branch as central motif, c. 1830. Photograph courtesy Corning Museum of Glass, Corning, New York* **2888** *Decanter with engraved eagle. Photograph courtesy Corning Museum of Glass, Corning, New York* **2889** *Carved pine pilothouse eagle. Photograph* **2890** *Glass goblet with engraved eagle and motto. Photograph courtesy Corning Museum of Glass, Corning, New York* **2891** *Cup plate with eagle. Probably from Boston & Sandwich Glass Works, 1831. Photograph courtesy Corning Museum of Glass, Corning, New York*

2889

2890   2891

2892   2893

2894   2895

2892–2897 *Coverlets woven 1800–1850. No single motif was repeated as often as the American eagle in nineteenth-century coverlets produced by both housewives and professional weavers. The eagle*

824

2896

sometimes occupied the central medallion but was
more often employed as a corner motif or repeated
figure in a border. Designs were derived from
weaving drafts that were exchanged throughout the
states

2897

2898

2899

2900

2901

UNITED STATES OF AMERICA

E PLURIBUS UNUM

1831

E PLURIBUS UNUM

CALISTA.C.JAMES
JEFFERSON.CO.N.Y.

1853

2898 *Damask weave in red and white which includes several patriotic slogans, the equestrian figure of Washington, and a border of eagles and stars. Made in New York state, 1841* **2899** *Reversible coverlet evidently made from the same weaving draft as that in 2898, though produced in Pennsylvania in 1842. Note how accidental weaving produced a double eagle in the border* **2900** *Bedspread with rare center medallion of the Great Seal* **2901** *Signature of the maker is linked with the eagle, ribbon, and* E Pluribus Unum, *1853*

Basket of Fruit with Flowers, *painted c. 1830 by an unknown New Jersey artist*

STATE
PROJECTS

ALABAMA: Montgomery

ARIZONA: Phoenix

CALIFORNIA

    Northern Division: San Francisco

    Southern Division: Los Angeles

COLORADO: Denver

CONNECTICUT: New Haven

DELAWARE: Wilmington

DISTRICT OF COLUMBIA:

    Washington

FLORIDA: Jacksonville

GEORGIA: Atlanta

ILLINOIS: Chicago

IOWA: Des Moines

KANSAS: Topeka

KENTUCKY: Louisville

LOUISIANA: New Orleans

MAINE: Portland

MARYLAND: Baltimore

MASSACHUSETTS: Boston

MICHIGAN: Lansing

MINNESOTA: St. Paul

MISSOURI: Jefferson City

NEW HAMPSHIRE: Manchester

NEW JERSEY: Newark

NEW MEXICO: Santa Fe

NEW YORK: Albany; New York City

NORTH CAROLINA: Raleigh

OHIO: Columbus

PENNSYLVANIA: Harrisburg

RHODE ISLAND: Providence

SOUTH CAROLINA: Columbia

TENNESSEE: Nashville

TEXAS: San Antonio

UTAH: Salt Lake City

VERMONT: Rutland

VIRGINIA: Richmond

WASHINGTON: Seattle

WISCONSIN: Madison

ARTISTS

Grant, D. J.
Harding, Donald
Henderer, Regina
Hukill, Henrietta S.
Jackson, Gwendolyn
Lawson, James M.
Loper, Edward L.
Macklem, Leslie J.
Miller, J.
Moll, John B.
Petrucci, John
Price, John
Rosel, Vincent
Saltar, Gordon
Swientochowski, John
Towers, E. A. Jr.
Wharry, Lawrence
White, Gould, *photographer*

DISTRICT
OF COLUMBIA
Montgomery, Mrs. Inez
Sterling, Ella Josephine
Stottlemeyer, Margaret
*Stelmach, *photographer*
Prince, Mildred

FLORIDA
Browne, Frank S.
Casaway, J. W.
Fossum, Magnus S.
Hassebrock, Fred
Holme, Maude
Johnston, Annie B.
Keane, Frank M.
Kelton, Maud S.
Merrill, Katherine
Parker, Cora
Runyan, Manuel G.
Walbeck, Alfred

Wilson, Carmel
Wilson, Marguerite

ILLINOIS
Aberdeen, Harry G.
Bates, Dorothea
Bevier, Milton
Blewett, Wellington
Bluhme, Oscar
Bodine, John
Brown, H. Langden
Buecher, Edward W.
Clark, Robert
Grossen, Harry
Kibbee, Edward
Koehl, John
Koehn, Alfred
Long, Louella
Ludwig, William
Mazur, Stanley
McCombs, Orrie
McEntee, Frank
Melzer, Kurt
Navigato, Rocco
Opstad, Adolph
Owen, Mary
Rekucki, Michael
Rudin, Albert
Spiecker, William
Thompson, Archie
Thorsen, John
Unger, Max
Vail, James H. C.
White, Wayne

IOWA
Bashaw, Edward
Brown, George C.
Davenport, F. C.

Dawson, Clarence W.
Diason, G. E.
Durand, Francis L.
Eiseman, Frank
Feidler, A.
Gilson, Robert
Golden, Margaret
Griffith, LeRoy
Hartenstein, Violet
Hightower, Herndon
Hollingsworth, Doris
Kempter, Harley
Marshall, Claude
Mason, Georgine
Merchant, Flora
Nelson, Lelah
Newmann, Raymond
Oldfield, Harold
Roberts, Sydney
Scalise, Gerald
Vernier, Racine

KANSAS
Ayres, Rolland W.
Clement, Clayton
Fritz, E. Allen
Fudge, Frank J.
Gray, Ethel Lillian
Greider, John F.
Henderson, Violet
Kent, M. Louise
Lockwood, Norma
Wear, Verna M., *photographer*

KENTUCKY
Brown, Mona
Carroll, Orville A.
Childers, William Paul
Cronk, Lon

Davidson, Mary C.
Goodwin, Charles Reed
Mowery, Elbert Samuel
Prater, Mary D.
Ulrich, Alois E.
Vezolles, George V.
Williams, Edward D.

LOUISIANA
Arbo, A.
Boyd, Joseph L.
Cannella, Joseph
Curry, Aldous R.
Doria, Alvin J.
Frère, Herbert S.
Mangelsdorf, Hans
Price, Ray
Verbeke, Lucien

MAINE
Avanzato, Dominic,
    photographer
Bartlett, Curry M.
Bent, Mildred
Davis, John
Gale, Harriette
Gray, Rosamond P.
Hentz, Karl J.
Poffinbarger, Paul
Skillin, Alton K.

MARYLAND
Alain, Marie
Arnold, Madeline
Bowman, Charles
Causey, Lillian
Campbell, Douglas
France, Michael
High, William
Meyer, George B.
Montgomery, Inez B.

Mosher, Steller
Philpot, Samuel
Schindele, C., *photographer*

MASSACHUSETTS
Berman, Sadie
Bilodeay, Laura
Broome, Lloyd
Chabot, Lucille
Cohen, Frances
Constantine, George
Cunningham, Eleanor
DeKalb, Beatrice
Dinghausen, Alfred
Domey, Alice
Dorr, Phyllis
*Fisher, *photographer*
Foster, Lawrence
Fuerst, Betty
Gale, Harriette
Ger, Anne
Gilman, Helen
Goldberg, Joseph
Hazen, Willard
Hyde, Hazel
Iverson, Jane
Kelleher, John W.
Koch, Gertrude
McIntyre, Samuel
Merrill, Sumner
Missirian, Zabelle
Moutal, Elizabeth
Muollo, Victor F.
Page, Marian
Peterson, Lawrence
Pollman, William
Rich, Winslow
Richards, A. J., *photographer*
Selmer-Larsen, Ingrid

Smith, Alfred H.
Smith, Irving I.
Stearns, Alice
Van Dunker, Dorothy
Wright, Wynna

MICHIGAN
Brennan, Dorothy
Bush, Rex
Chichester, Beverly
Coleman, Anne
Croe, Eugene
File, George F.
Gray, Frank
Harris, Dorothy
Hiatt, Helmle, *photographer*
Hochstrasser, Walter
Makrenos, Chris
McLellan, James
Ramage, David
Rokita, Florian
Stahl, Lillian
Strzalkowski, Edward
Vance, Vivian L.
Weise, Elmer

MINNESOTA
Heiberg, Einar
Keksi, Karl
Luedke, Mrs. Gene
Quackenbush, Lloyd
Rice, Wilbur
Sharp, Floyd R.

MISSOURI
Barnett, Gerard
Brooks, Adele
Chomyk, Michael
Clement, Clayton
Erganian, Sarkis

835

Ficcadenti, J.
Finley, William
Gutting, Frank W.
Hagen, Emil
Haupt, Dolores
Kelly, Paul
King, Harry
Makimson, Loraine
Rigsby, Robert
Ritchey, Lionel
Walsh, Hardin D.
Weisenborn, Harold
Williams, Donald
Turnbull, James B.

NEW HAMPSHIRE
Cosgrove, Alice
Herrick, Marion E.
Lacoursière, Lucille
Lewis, Ralph M.

NEW JERSEY
Bernhardt, George
Brush, Julie C.
Buergernaise, Carl
Calderon, Ludmilla
Camilli, Albert
Connin, Peter
Cutting, John
Durand, Francis L.
Famularo, Marie
Fischer, L. Valdemar
Gaskill, Marion
Hall, John
Halpin, Grace
Klein, Samuel O.
Holloway, Thomas
Jennings, Walter W.
Magnette, Edith

Manupelli, Raymond
*Marsh
McIntyre, Marjorie
Meyers, Henry
Miller, Edith
Moon, Roy
Murphy, Vincent
Nelson, Frank
O'Neill, J. J.
Papa, Joseph
Pearce, E. L.
Schuerer, Robert
Schwabe, Erwin
Shane, Charles R.
Simpson, Columeris
Sudek, Joseph
Stevenson, F.
Streeter, Donald
Taylor, Richard
Ward, Paul
Wegg, Arthur
Zuccarello, A.

NEW MEXICO
Barrio, Conrado
Boyd, E.
Claflin, Majel G.
Lantz, Juanita
Marley, J. Henry
Mirabal, Alfonso
Parish, Margery
Reimer, Richard
Thomas, Grace
Wiswall, Etna

NEW YORK CITY
Acampora, Nicholas
Almgren, Jenny
Amantea, Nicholas

Annino, L.
Bader, Herman
Beer, Doris
Benge, Jessie M.
Berge, Virginie
Berner, Mary
Bialostosky, Ruth
Borelli, Francis
Borrazzo, Salvatore
Boyd, Julia
Budash, Frank
Burzy, Vincent
Campbell, Rollington
Capaldo, Ernest
Capelli, Gianito
Carano, Vincent
Cartier, Ferdinand
Caseau, Charles
Choate, F.
Clark, Mae A.
Colgan, J. N.
Concha, Margaret
Cook, Gladys
Crimi, Nancy
Curtiss, Marion
Dana, John
Danziger, Isador
Delasser, Yolande
Dezon, Sylvia
De Wolfe, Henry
Dieterich, John
Doran, Walter
Drozdoff, Leo
Duany, Hester
Dwin, Dorothy
Eisman, H.
Emanuel, H.
Fairchild, Elizabeth

Fastovsky, Aaron
Fenge, M.
Ford, Mildred
Forman, Bessie
Fowler, Catherine
Frankes, P.
Fulda, Elisabeth
Fumagalli, Frank
Garfinkel, Sara
Gernon, Dorothie
Gibbes, Winifred
Gilsleider, Edward J.
Goldberg, Isidore
Gordon, Jean
Granet, Henry
Greene, Minna
Grubstein, Milton
Gussow, Bernard
Hansen, Esther
Harnly, Perkins
Henning, Charles
Herrett, Emery
Hobert, Helen
Hoffman, Melita
Johnson, Arthur
Johnson, Philip
Karlin, Agnes
Kieran, Dorothy
Lacey, Dorothy
Lane, Rosalia
Larzelere, Fanchon
Lassen, Ben
Lawson, Irene
Le Fevere, Jules Z.
Lemberg, Gertrude
Lindermayor, John
Lipkin, J.
Livingston, Rolland

Loughridge, George
Lowry, Mina
Lubrano, Joseph
Maralian, A.
Marshack, Daniel
May, Ada V.
McBride, Hubbell
Mierisch, Dorothea
Middleton, Owen
Mitchell, Marie
Mose, Eric
Mosseller, Lillian M.
Nason, Alfred
Perkins, Arlene
Peszel, Jean
Phillips, L.
Pimentel, Palmyra
Resnick, Benjamin
Riza, Janet
Rothenberg, Joseph
Rothkranz, L.
Roy, Suzanne
Ruelos, Eleanor
Sackerman, Gilbert
Sanborn, Gordon
Sandler, Selma
Shiren, Alvin
Silvay, Van
Sovensky, Isidor
Spicer, Joel
Squeres, C.
Staloff, Jack
Steinberg, Isidore
Szilvasy, May
Tarantino, John
Tercuzzi, John H.
Trekur, Michael
Tuccio, Amelia

Van Felix, Maurice
Von-Paulin, M. Rosenschield
Von Urban, Charles,
    photographer
Walton, Kalamein
Wenger, F.
Westmacott, Bernard
Winter, Charlotte
Zaidenberg, A.

NEW YORK STATE

Badin, Ferdinand
Brown, E.
Cavanaugh, John
De Strange, Isabella
De Vault, David S.
Earl, F.
Fitzgerald, Mary
Fletcher, D.
Gausser, E.
Gibbo, Pearl
Glover, Joseph
Lumbard, Howard N.
Luttrell, M.
Matthews, Arthur
Merkley, Arthur G.
Parker, Cushman
Phillips, G.
Plogsted, Louis
Sanborn, Gordon
Schmid, M.
Schmidt, W.
Scrymser, C.
Shearwood, William P.
Sherlock, Geneviere M.
Spangenbergh, G.
Topolosky, A.
Watts, Thomas
Whitaker, R.
Youngs, Jesse M.

Zito, Emilio

OHIO

Barnett, Richard
Boehmer, Fritz
Bronson, Helen
Bulone, Angelo
Cline, Orville
Dadante, Michael
Drake, James
Dyball, Adelaide
Graham, Ernest, *photographer*
Guinta, Jerry
Jennings, Harry
Larson, Carol
Russell, Ralph
Wilkes, John

PENNSYLVANIA

Anderson, Elmer G.
Angus, Charlotte
Antrim, William L.
Brown, Roy S.
Buergernaiss, Carl
Calbick, William, *photographer*
Davis, Betty Jean
Davison, Austin L.
Dingman, Bryon
Fleming, Elmo
Gross, James, *photographer*
Hays, Mrs. May, *photographer*
Iams, J. Howard
Jean, Albert
Kottcamp, Elmer R.
Levone, Albert Jean
Lichten, Frances
McGough, Raymond
Mitry, Joseph
McComb, Inez
Moran, Henry

Moss, Charles, *photographer*
Newswanger, Myra
Ogle, Charles, *photographer*
Poster, D.
Roadman, Charles
Shellady, Eugene
Soltmann, Max
Strehlau, Carl
Syres, Franklyn
Wenrich, Luther D.
White, Edward
Wilson, Eva
Weber, Roy

RHODE ISLAND

Barton, Robert
Donovan, Donald
Gold, Albert
Handy, Dorothy
Murphy, Henry
Pohle, Robert
Riccitelli, Michael
Ryder, Albert
Sullivan, J.
Tomaszewski, Henry

SOUTH CAROLINA

Gordon, Margaret

TEXAS

Bolser, G.
Brennan, Joe, Jr.
Davis, Pearl
Gomez, Rafaela
Guerra, Flora G.
Guillaudeu, Gladys M.
Johnson, Dorothy E.
Lauderdale, Ursula
Liberto, Virgil A.
Molina, Esther

Pena, Jesus
Rivero, R.
Starr, Angela
Ustinoff, Peter C.

UTAH

Cheney, Clyde L.
Mace, Frank J.
Martindale, Esther
Rosenbaum, Howell
Shurtliff, Wilford H.
Smith, Cecil
Truelson, Florence M.

VERMONT

Lovett, Cleo

VIRGINIA

Alward, Linnet
Bodenstein, Molly
Brown, Florence Grant
Burton, Mary Ann
Busey, Rosa G.
Darby, Edward A.
Eubank, Ann Belle
Farrington, Dorothea
Gills, Robert
Goodman, Mattie
Grant, Florence H.
Humes, Mary E.
Ions, Willoughby
Jones, Mamie M.
Kennady, Virginia
Monfalcone, Renee
Pettijohn, Lucille
Powell, Francis W.
Raike, Elizabeth
Rex, Edna
Skeen, Jesse
Styll, Elgin M.

Vaughan, Annie L.

WASHINGTON
Bruseth, Alf
Correll, Richard
Fletcher, William O.
Fossek, Clementine
Haugland, Augustine

WISCONSIN
Anderson, Alexander
*Ballard
Bartz, Eugene
*Beck

*Bernhardt
Biehn, Irving L.
*Daeda
Dooley, Thomas
Faigin, Samuel
Fallon, Michael
Fernekes, Max
Frank, William
Geuppert, Albert
Gielens, Jacob
Lang, William
*Lauterbach
Lemcke, Lloyd Charles

Miller, Eugene C.
Moreno, Alfonso
Praefke, Walter
*Roehl
Secor, Clarence
Stenzel, Erwin
Stroh, Herman O.
Tardiff, Robert
*Thoss
*Volem
Waldeci, H.

INDEX

The design as well as the text of these volumes
is the work of Clarence P. Hornung, who also created
the typographic format, marginal decorations,
and binding design. The type is set in Times Roman
with initial letters and book titles in the author's Georgian
initials; the chapter headings were hand-set by him
in Caslon italic swash letters.